Getting the Web

Getting the Web

Understanding the Nature and Meaning of the Internet

Jeanne M. Follman

Stafford Library
Columbia College
1001 Rogers Street
Columbia, Missouri 65216

Duomo Press
CHICAGO

Published by Duomo Press
Chicago, IL
www.duomopress.com

Copyright © 2001 by Jeanne M. Follman

All rights reserved. Except as permitted under the Copyright Act of 1976, no part of this publication may be reproduced or distributed in any form or by any means or stored in a database or retrieval system, without the written permission of the publisher.

Product and company names mentioned herein may be trademarks of their respective owners. Their use does not imply any affiliation, connection, or endorsement of the products or their owners.

Printed and bound in the United States of America.

Publisher's Cataloging In Publication

Follman, Jeanne M.
   Getting the Web : understanding the nature and meaning of the Internet / by Jeanne M. Follman. -- 1st ed.
   p. cm.
   Includes bibliographical references and index.
   LCCN: 00-190979
   ISBN: 0-9679456-9-0

   1. Internet. 2. World Wide Web. 3. Telecommunication. I. Title.

TK5105.875.I57F65 2001   384.3'3
                    QBI00-854

Cover graphic derived from NASA photo STS040-077-044
Courtesy National Aeronautics and Space Administration

Cover design by JACQUELYN GRAPHICS
www.jacquelyngraphics.com

To Liz and Clare

Table of Contents

The Big Picture — 13
- Looking at What, Not How — 14
- Structure of the Book — 16

Part I

The Telephone Company for Computers — 21
- Computers — 22
- The Telephone Network — 27
- Clients and Servers — 27
- Summary: The Telephone Company for Computers — 30

Files — 32
- Signals — 32
- Suck It and See — 33

Files of Words — 35
- Visualizing Discourse — 36
- *A Changing Relationship with Text*
  - Mesopotamia dot COM — 37
  - The Solitary Reader — 39
  - The Logic of the Book — 40
- *The Flavor of Text on the Internet*
  - Hypertext – Connection Made Manifest — 42
  - Breaking Down Barriers — 43
  - What We Were After All Along? — 43

Files of Pictures — 45
- Image File Guts - Pictures as 0s and 1s — 46
- Pictures are Cool — 47
- Visual Knowledge — 48
- Photographs — 49
- Art — 50

Files of Sound and Motion — 52

Sound as 0s and 1s 52
Streaming Audio 53
MP3 54
Internet Radio 56
Broadcasting Internet Radio 58
Video on the Web 59

Files of Logic — 61

Smart Servers 62
Smart Servers - Business to Business 65
Smart Clients 66
Downloading Programs 66
The Telephone Company for Computers 67

Part II

Open Standards — 71

Standards and Communication 71
File Types 72
File Standards 73
Standards and the Birth of the Web 73
Standards Today 74
Open Standards 75
Open vs. Proprietary Standards 76
Open Standards and Growth 77
The Power of Cooperation 78

Searching the Web — 80

Push vs. Pull 82
Catalogs, Search Engines, and Portals 83
Mechanizing Meaning 85
Metadata 86
Sort of Meta 87
Real Metadata 88

Bandwidth and the World Wide Wait   91
The Local Loop 92
The Internet 95
The Internet Service Provider (ISP) 96
Traffic on the Internet 96
Bandwidth 97
Speeding up the Internet Network 99
Speeding Up the Local Loop 100
In the Interim 101
Speed in Both Directions 102
Broadband Solutions
   Asymmetric Digital Subscriber Line (ADSL)
      and the Poor, Deaf Phone Company 103
   Cable TV.. 105
   Fiber Optics 106
   Wireless Options 106
Accessibility Issues 107
Cost and Convergence 108
Why Bandwidth Matters 108

Content and Connection   111
Bundling 111
Bundling in a Broadband World 112
Bundling Access and ISPs 113
Public Networks Connect 115
Content, Connection and Convergence 115
History Repeats Itself 116
The Pricing Issue 117
The Infrastructure Challenge 118

Part III

Individuals in Conversation   121
Communication and Exchange 121
The Power of Publishing 123

The Power To Exchange 124
  The Creator's Tool of Choice 124
  Using Files for Communication and Exchange 125
  Visualizing Discourse 127
  Internet Time.. 128
  Discourse and the Shaping of Content.................................. 129
  Sharing and Amplifying Intellectual Capital 130

Formation of Community   **132**

  Conveying Presence 133
  Reaching the Niche Audience 134
  A Small Corner of Cyberspace 135
  Victorian Email 135
  Enhancing Physical Communities 136
  The Virtual Corporation 137
  The Community that Created the Internet 138
  Doing Good and Showing Off.. 138
  Open Source 139
  Transparency and Complexity 140
  Cyberspace is Earth 141

Conversations Driving Change   **143**

  The Free Flow of Information 144
  Access Changes Structure 145
  Everyone's an Operator 147
  The Price in the Marketplace.. 147
  The Marketplace Itself 148
  A Market of One... 149

An Outbreak of Sanity   **151**

  Illumination and Formalization 152
  Transparency.. 153
  Epiphanies of Context 155
  Welcome to the Renaissance 157

Glossary   **161**
Bibliography   **167**
Index   **169**

Earthrise

Photo: National Aeronautics and Space Administration

The Big Picture

IT'S BEEN AN interesting millennium – the past one that is. And while we've had our share of horrors, the gifts have been substantial: democracy, freedom of speech, equal rights, concern for our environment, and that first lovely picture of Earth taken from the Moon by the Apollo 8 astronauts. Apollo 8 was the first manned mission to the Moon. Astronauts Frank Borman, Jim Lovell, and William Anders entered lunar orbit on Christmas Eve, December 24, 1968; that evening, they did a live television broadcast from orbit that showed the famous Earthrise over the barren lunar landscape. Lovell said, "The vast loneliness is awe-inspiring and it makes you realize just what you have back there on Earth." They ended the broadcast with the crew taking turns reading from the book of Genesis. Borman then added, "And from the crew of Apollo 8, we close with good night, good luck, a Merry Christmas, and God bless all of you – all of you on the good Earth."

Two weeks later, the seeds of the Internet were planted when the U.S. Department of Defense sent out a Request For Proposal for a computer network. In the final five years of the last millennium, that computer network blossomed across the planet as the Internet and the World Wide Web. The picture of Earth taken by the Apollo 8 astronauts forever changed the way we think about ourselves. The Internet is now irrevocably changing the way in which we interact, launching us into the new millennium with the tools to create the next renaissance.

The gift of the Internet and the Web is this – it offers to each individual the powers of communication and exchange that in the past were held only by governments and corporations:

- The power to publish complex repositories of thought and visual representations of knowledge, image and art.
- The power to broadcast music, radio and video and to publish software.
- The power to do business with a global market.
- The power to carry on global conversations and to form communities of knowledge and interest.
- The power to shape institutions to serve the individuals who give them meaning.

The challenge will be understanding enough about the Internet and the Web to fully participate in this phenomenon and to have a voice in deciding where it is taking us as a society.

The good news is that in order to do this, to *get the Web*, we really only have to understand what it is, not how it works.

Looking at What, Not How

I only vaguely understand how my car works: It has something to do with carburetors, pistons and crankshafts. But I have a very clear understanding of what my car is: a machine that I can drive over the roads to get from one place to another. So while *how* it works is mostly a mystery, the idea of *what* my car is allows me to use it just fine. I know it doesn't fly or jump fences; I know I must keep it on the road and I know the rules of the road; I get the idea. Clearly a lack of technical automotive knowhow has not stopped me or anyone else from using automobiles. It also hasn't stopped us from entering civic debates about appropriate uses, ranging from who should be granted drivers licenses to disputes over road construction to public policy decisions on roads vs. mass transit. Likewise, the lack of a technical understanding of electronic publishing, prepress, printing and binding doesn't keep us from debates about books. We know what a book is and this knowledge gives us the wherewithal to participate in important discussions on literacy, censorship, and freedom of the press.

The *how* of the Internet is marvelously complex, a shining achievement not only of technology but of international cooperation. The Web came into existence thanks to Tim Berners-Lee, the English gent who defined the standards and protocols of the Web. It also came into existence thanks to that huge and ever-growing group of people who each individually agree to make their computers act in the standardized fashion that enables the serving and browsing of the words, pictures, sound, and motion that make up the Web. But *how* is not what this book is about. There are hundreds of fine books that already explain the how of it much better than I ever could. This book is about the *what*: what is the Internet and specifically what is the Web. My goal is to give you as clear an understanding as I can of the *what* of the Web, so that you may use it to your best advantage as well as fully entering the civic debate on where the Web is going and how to best realize its full potential.

And it isn't all that difficult. Happily, despite the mind-blowing complexity of the *how* of the Web, the *what* of the Web is straightforward. If you've used a computer, know what a file is, have surfed a bit and are familiar with telephones, you know all that you need to know to benefit from this book. And you can always consult the Glossary at the back of the book if you find a term whose meaning is unclear. After reading this book, you should be better able to get what's happening on the Web and participate in deciding where this golden technology is taking us.

Structure of the Book

In Part I, we look at what the Internet is: the telephone company for computers. We also describe what happens when individuals exchange words, pictures, sound, motion, and logic by putting them in files and moving them back and forth on the Web.

Part II explores why the Internet is the way it is: how computers and telephone networks shape the nature of the Internet. We see how open standards successfully orchestrate the daily movement of millions of files, we look at search engines, we see why bandwidth is an issue, and we explore the crucial difference in a public network between content and connection.

In Part III, we discuss the ways in which the Internet shapes communication and exchange and ultimately, us. The Internet gives us a splendid mechanism to hold an enriched conversation or to do business with anyone on the planet. And when people start talking on the Internet, information flows freely, anyone can publish, barriers to entry for many businesses are virtually eliminated, intellectual capital increases, feedback shapes content, communities of interest gain voice, local communities thrive, and complex and differentiated entities form and emerge, like the open source movement and the Internet itself. Information illuminates. The Internet will make obvious new ways of doing things and create new ways of looking at life. With it, we can more easily see ourselves in the full context of who we really are and ensure that our institutions truly function the way they should.

છે.

"Internet" and "Web" are key words in this book. The Web is the part of the Internet that you see when you're surfing and clicking on links. If you're sending an email, you're still using the Internet but you're not on the Web. The Web is the most popular

THE BIG PICTURE

part of the Internet, the part that brought it into public consciousness, and the part that's driving its enormous growth.

❧

The Internet is the technology that will forever change the way in which we interact, offering us a forum for communication and exchange with potentially any person on the planet. But what exactly is it, and why has it saturated the Earth in such a short time? The Internet is the telephone company for computers. Telephone networks and computers have been around for quite some time. The building blocks were there, just awaiting connection. And when we figured out how to put them together in an open, transparent way, we gave birth to the Internet.

GETTING THE WEB

Part I

Part I of the book explains what the Internet is – the telephone company for computers. It also describes the files that move back and forth on the Web (files of words, pictures, sound and motion, and files of logic) and what we can do with them.

GETTING THE WEB

The Telephone Company for Computers

WITH ONE COMPUTER and a phone line, as Supreme Court Justice John Paul Stevens put it, a person's voice can resonate around the world. Of course your voice can resonate around the world with a telephone alone, but only to the person you happen to call. However, when you stick a computer at the end of your telephone, it opens an entirely new realm of communication. You can pack an enormous number of words into a computer; much more than you can into a telephone conversation. You can add pictures, sound, and motion. You can make it interactive. And you can make it accessible to millions of people anywhere in the world at any time of the day or night.

In the video *Nerds 2.0.1: A Brief History of the Internet*, Apple Computer's Steve Jobs says that "the Internet morphs the computer from a computation device to a device for communication." Individuals have heaped computers to the brim with files of words, pictures, sound, motion, and logic. And like a planet full of exuberant teenagers with phones hanging out of their ears, millions of our computers now have modems hanging out of their ears. With the Internet, computers now have a way to share.

But what is the Internet? The Internet is the telephone company for computers; it's what happened when telecommunications and computers, two huge industries that had been thriving in parallel for decades, finally reached out, touched one another, and exploded across the planet. Go figure. A machine created to crank numbers and a telephone network specifically designed to transmit an analog signal of the human voice have become the brains and blood of the digital communication tool of the new millennium.

The best way to understand the Internet is to think first about the basic natures of computers and the telephone network, both of which are familiar to us. If you get the nature of computers and telephone networks and then put the two together, you're well on your way to *Getting the Web*.

First let's look at computers.

Computers

Humans communicate and create art by arranging things or causing them to move around: clay on a tablet, ink on a page, paint on a canvas, bodies on a stage, sound waves in the air. Now we have a new thing to move around: bits, the 0s and 1s we use to create meaning in computing.

Here's how you use bits to say "Hello" in English as encoded using the American Standard Code for Information Interchange (ASCII), a code for translating numbers and letters into bits:

01001000 01100101 01101100 01101100 01101111

If you had a digitized picture of the ancestral farm in Ireland, it would also look like a long string of 0s and 1s. If you had some digitized Mozart, it too would look like a long string of 0s and 1s. And if you had some cyber-aromatherapy (which we don't have yet but if we did), it would look like a long string of 0s and 1s.

Looking at bits is a lot like looking at life at the atomic level; when you get low enough, everything looks about the same. Bits are a lovely medium because they are so elemental and so infinitely combinable. Neurons, protons and electrons arrange to create elements, molecules, and various life forms such as ourselves. Likewise, bits can be arranged in files to create digitized representations of just about anything, including words, pictures, sound and motion, as well as the logic of computer programming. The building blocks are simple, just 0s and 1s, but they can be combined in an infinite number of ways, in files of virtually any size, giving us a communications medium of tremendous scope and pliability.

And how do we make sense of all those 0s and 1s? Through standards. In computers, as in life, there is no meaning without context, and standards create the context for the streams of bits in files. ASCII, one of the standards for representing text, defines specific bit streams for each number, letter, and special character in the standard:

```
H = 01001000
e = 01100101
l = 01101100
l = 01101100
o = 01101111
```

The ASCII standard, plus the fact that a computer program knows that a file is an ASCII file in the first place, allows it to read the bit streams correctly and to pop the words onto your monitor.

A standard defines each file type that you have on your computer or see on the Internet; thousands of people worldwide occupy themselves by developing and enhancing these standards. For example, a new standard for wireless Internet access, the Wireless Access Protocol (WAP), has recently been agreed upon, enabling a common language for surfing from cellular phones or hand-held devices. If we ever get cyber-aromatherapy on the Web, it will be because some group created a digital standard for scents, put digitized smell files that follow the standard on a server, and created a product that uses the files to render the smell in a way accessible to the human nose. Imagine the possibilities: Irish cottage turf fire, Venetian canal sludge, backyard hostas in bloom, Parisian early morning coffee and fresh-baked bread. If a thing can be represented digitally in a standardized manner and then converted back so we can see, hear, smell, touch, or taste it, eventually it could end up on the Internet.

Bits are one of the things on the planet that we're not going to run out of any time soon. Via computers, bits provide a means with reasonable effort to permanently store words, pictures, sound and motion so they will not be lost to memory. Nobody's going to chip the more than half a million definitions in the twenty volumes of the Oxford English Dictionary into stone, but they did get them into a computer; the entire OED fits on one compact disk. And we now measure storage devices in gigabytes (i.e., billions of characters) rather than megabytes (millions). With bits in computers, we have a communications medium that is relatively easy to use and contains a storage capacity approaching the infinite. This means that you can not only store vast amounts of words, pictures, sound and motion in a computer, you can add to it and elaborate on it over time, creating works of amazing complexity.

Complexity, a key and most annoying characteristic of computers, used to just drive programmers nuts; now everyone gets to struggle with it. But complexity is also enabling. As psychologist Erik Erikson has said, "Complexity is the soul's oxygen; it is what enables us to be fully, radiantly human." Complexity both enables and drives evolution. Sometimes, when a thing gets too complex it just breaks. But if it gets complex in a well-formed manner, it enables the breakthrough to an entirely new level of creation. That's what we've seen with the Internet and the Web. The computer's ability to harbor complex arrangements of bits has provided a way for people to have enriched conversations and generate all kinds of astounding products, services, and information in a remarkably short period of time.

Even though computers offer vast storage and vast complexity with any number of ways to represent digital information, there are still some basic rules. A key one is this: Everything at some point or another ends up in a file. Each word-processing document or spreadsheet on your computer is a file. Likewise, the words, pictures, sound and motion that you see on the Web are each also stored in their own files. And it is these files in transit that make up the traffic on the Internet.

But until it gets on the Internet, what is on your computer is for your eyes only unless you drag someone over to view your monitor, arrange to put it on a local area network, or print it out and pass it around. The boom in junk mail and the popularity of xerox and fax machines attest to the potent need, once a person or a corporation has collected a vast store of information, to share that information with its victims. Picture a planet full of people with computers bursting with data just waiting to be shared, using the inefficient means of print and xerox. You can then begin to appreciate the pent-up energy that the Internet has released.

Besides managing all those words and pictures, computers still spend a lot of their time doing the job they did when they were first invented: They compute. Adding up your credit card transactions, cranking spreadsheet numbers, managing air traffic information, switching your telephone calls, telling you that your door is ajar, and printing paychecks, computers excel at manipulating information. As the Internet grows more sophisticated, computers will not only share files with one another but will also share computation.

One of the coolest examples of this is a project underway run by SETI, the Search for Extraterrestrial Intelligence (setiathome.ssl.berkeley.edu). Called SETI@Home, this project distributes processing of radio telescope data. Just a few months after it launched, the project had signed up over a million volunteers in 200 countries. As a volunteer, you download a chunk of recorded radio telescope data as well as a program to process it. When the processing is done, the program takes you to the Web site to return the processed data and get another chunk. The program runs as a screen saver while your computer is inactive, analyzing data in the background. The analysis of radio telescope data requires a huge amount of processing power and would normally be the type of application run on a supercomputer. However, distributing the task to volunteers provides access to almost limitless power at practically no cost. From the volunteer point of view, it's sort of like joining an electronic quilting bee. You become a part of a team working as a group to make a contribution to science. And you get a cool screen saver to boot.

With its marriage of computing and communication, the Internet is a perfect venue for the distribution of processing across a wide number of computers, generating a level of computational power far greater than any supercomputer could provide. When we think of the Internet from now on, we should think not only in terms of using our browsers to surf; we should also think of using our browsers to run other programs. Some of the most interesting Internet experiences of the future will be via the execution of programs, and not just the SETI flavor of borrowing your computer's processing power. It will be through programs that allow us to have conversations with another person or organization in an increasingly complex and customized fashion. It will also allow organizations to interact with each other in the same complex and customized fashion.

The Telephone Network

The physical network that comprises the Internet is slowly evolving into its own distinct self but much of it (and all of it in the beginning) was piggybacked on the existing telephone voice network. That was good, because by the time the Internet came along, the telephone network circled the Earth. What wasn't good was the fact that the telephone network was engineered from the beginning to carry an analog signal representing sound in the 300-3300 cycle per second range, just right for the human voice, but lousy for the transmission of bits. The entire structure upon which the Internet rests was designed for something else entirely. That is why even today surfing can be so slow; we're using the telephone network for something for which it wasn't designed. But that's what we have so that's what we use, until such a time as we all get high-speed, broadband access to the Internet.

Because the Internet evolved on the telephone network, it has these characteristics: it goes everywhere to everyone, it goes slowly, and like all communication, it follows the model of a *sender*, a *signal*, and a *receiver*.

Clients and Servers

Every telephone has a mouth piece and an ear piece. When you talk on the telephone, your voice goes from the transmitter (i.e., sender) in the mouthpiece, through the network, to the ear piece (i.e., receiver) in the telephone of the person to whom you are talking.

The communication has these parts:

- Sender - the mouth piece
- Signal - the sound of the conversation
- Receiver - the ear piece

On the Internet, it's the same:

- Sender - the server
- Signal - the file
- Receiver - the client

Servers and clients go as happily together as mouth pieces and ear pieces in telephones, only instead of sending and receiving the human voice, they send and receive files filled with our words and pictures. However, surfing is mostly a one-way street: when we surf, we receive. Web *browsers* like Netscape Navigator and Microsoft Internet Explorer are client programs because they are mostly in the business of receiving (i.e., browsing) files.

In a telephone conversation, one person talks, the network carries the signal, and the other person hears the voice. On the Internet, a person who is surfing asks for a file over the network by clicking on a link in a browser. This causes a file to travel across the network from the server to the person's computer. Instead of sending a signal that represents a human voice going from one person to another, the telephone company for computers sends a signal that represents a file going from server software on one computer to client software on another computer.

- Client - the receiver - a software program whose function is to *download* (i.e., obtain) files from a distant server and display or play them so they can be seen or heard. For example, a Web browser is a client software program that downloads and displays Web files from all over the planet.

- File - the signal - a collection of bits that form the content of the communication. Bits can represent words, pictures, sound, motion, and logic. For example, each picture in a Web page is a file, as is the Web page itself.
- Server - the sender - a software program whose function is to present files so they can be obtained by clients.

Servers serve digitally and files transmit digitally. But once it gets to your computer, the bits in those files have to be converted back to something you can see or hear (we haven't gotten to smell, touch, or taste yet) and that is also the job of the client. The client converts that digital stream into something accessible to the human senses, just as a telephone receiver converts electrical signals into sound. Client software must render words, pictures and motion on a monitor so we can see it, or create sound in a speaker so we can hear it. In all cases, the digital files served define the words, pictures, sound or motion and the client software understands the file formats and renders the transmission properly.

For every standard type of file, you need server software and client software. The original client on the Web was the browser. It first displayed the text and image files of which Web pages are constructed, served by the Web's original server software. As developers invented new types of files for the Web such as audio and video files, they also developed both server software and client software so that audio and video files could be served and played. Sometimes the client is a separate program; sometimes it is a small program called a *plug-in* that plays the file from within the browser.

Here are some typical clients, and the types of files they can display and play:

- Web browsers like Netscape Navigator and Microsoft

Internet Explorer can play Web page files as well as image files. With the proper plug-ins they can also play sound and video files and execute files of logic.
- Audio and video players such as QuickTime and RealPlayer can play audio and video files.
- Email clients, news group clients, instant messaging clients and chat clients can both display files as well as send files back via a server for others to see.

To create a new way to communicate on the Internet, you need three basic components: the definition of a standard file type, software that serves the standard file type, and software that plays the standard file type. If it's happening on the Internet, it's a client, a server, or a file.

Summary: The Telephone Company for Computers

The Internet uses the telephone network to move files from servers to clients:

- A person serves a file on a computer using server software.
- The files contain representations of words, pictures, sound, motion, and logic that are defined by standards and can be of vast number, size, and complexity. Traffic on the network consists of files moving between servers and clients; the network goes everywhere and everyone on it can reach everyone else.
- A person uses client software, like a browser, to download a file from a server. The client renders the bits in the file into something the person can see or hear.

It's the telephone company for computers.

THE TELEPHONE COMPANY FOR COMPUTERS

The concept of "telephone company" is changing today from a wired network to a mix of wired and wireless cell phones, while the concept of "computer" is changing to include mini-laptop and palm-held devices and cell phones. The concept of "Internet" is changing accordingly. If you talk on your cell phone, despite the fact that your voice is traveling through the air rather than a wire, you know you're still talking on a phone. After a while it feels perfectly normal. Likewise, once you get used to it, it will seem perfectly normal to check weather, traffic, or stock quote Web sites via your new cell phone that has a small text display above the number pad. So even though you're using a phone, you're still surfing in a recognizable manner:

- Instead of surfing from your computer, you surf and email from your cell phone client that contains logic and acts like a computer.
- Instead of a set of files that represent words, pictures, sound and motion, you download a text-only file.
- Instead of serving a full Web site, only special text files are served.

Imagine a world of teenagers chatting in chat rooms and sending instant messages and smiley-faces from cell phones; it's already happened in Europe and Japan. How about Internet radio on your cell phone or (my personal favorite) karaoke on demand? It doesn't matter how the files are served and transmitted, or from where: peer-to-peer technologies will allow serving (ala Napster) direct from your own hard disk. It doesn't matter what the client looks like. Digital devices and transmission networks may change, but the same framework holds true. A client pulls a file from a server, and the file holds the message, which is the heart of the communication.

Files

Signals

YOU KNOW what a file is. Each word processing document or spreadsheet in your computer is a file composed of 0s and 1s and defined by a particular standard file format (e.g., AppleWorks 5.0, Excel 97, Word 97). Anything in motion or at rest on the Internet is also a file composed of 0s and 1s and defined by a particular Internet file standard. Even though a file is broken up into pieces (i.e., *packets*) for transmission across the network, it is both served as a file on the server and then pasted back together again so it can be played or displayed by the client. Sometimes the entire file has to arrive before it can be played; sometimes the beginning of the file can be played as the rest of it downloads. Nevertheless, the basic unit of communication on the Internet is the file.

On the Internet, the file is the signal. Like a voice over a phone line, it goes from the sender (the server) to the receiver (the client). Regardless of whether the 0s and 1s represent words, pictures, sound, motion, or anything else, the file is the signal that contains the message.

Suck It and See

You can find any file on the Web as long as there's a link to it: the typically blue, underlined text or the image that generates the little pointing finger in your browser. Links use an address called a URL (Uniform Resource Locator) that defines the location of the server itself on the Internet as well as the location of the file on the server. The act of clicking on a link tells your browser to use the associated URL to find that file and suck it down to your computer so your browser or other client can display or play it for you. Therefore, every time you click on a link, you affect a series of file transfers from servers anywhere in the world to your machine so you can view them. After you click on a link your computer has more files on it than it did before you clicked.

Clicking on a link on the Internet is like making a phone call on a telephone network; the URL associated with the link is the equivalent of the phone number of the file.

The URL tells you two key pieces of information: the location of the server on the Internet and the location of the file on the server. Specifically, the URL tells you:

- the type of protocol (e.g., http for the Web)
- the domain name (e.g., duomopress.com), which translates to a physical network address identifying the location of the server
- the path of folders or directories within the server in which the file can be found
- the name of the file

Here's a URL:

http://www.mozartrules.com/piano/sonatas/K545.html

It tells you that the file can be read by a Web browser (http) and that the domain name of the server is mozartrules.com. Using this domain name, the network can physically locate the server on the Internet. Then the URL tells you that the file "K545.html" is in the folder "sonatas" which is in the folder "piano" in the "www" area of the server. Because of the URL, when you click

GETTING THE WEB

on a link, the Internet can locate the exact file related to that link. When you click on the link, your browser sends a message to the server requesting that file. As you patiently wait, the network transfers the file to your computer and your browser displays its contents on your monitor.

If it's on the Internet, you can look at it, hear it, or (one day) smell it because a client has requested a file from a server and then played that file for you. The Internet is the telephone company for computers. Traffic on the Internet is no more or no less than billions of requests and files, flying back and forth all over the world, between clients that have requested the files and servers that have served them.

ε●

Now let's look at the types of files we find on the Web and see what they contain.

Files of Words

Too much of a good thing is wonderful.

– Mae West

IN EMAILS, chat rooms, Web pages, news groups and instant messages, countless words fly across the Internet every day; the written word hasn't seen such a boost since the invention of printing.

We have been storing our thoughts in various forms of writing for about five thousand or six thousand years. In each case (as with telephones and computers) there is a sender, a signal, and a receiver. The signal can be pressed into clay, chipped into stone, written on a papyrus, inscribed on parchment made from the skin of an animal, printed in a book or newspaper, or squirted in pixels on the screen of a computer monitor. The point is the communication of a message. It can be anything from an accounting entry, to a stock quote, to the conveyance of an entire world created in one person's imagination and given life in another's: Sherlock Holmes, Winnie the Pooh, Hamlet, Star Wars, or Star Trek (OK, those last two are visual media but the books keep us going in between the movies and the episodes).

In his book *The History and Power of Writing*, Henri-Jean Martin says the following about how we encode our thoughts in writing systems:

> The signs that were aligned by the human hand were

nothing by themselves. What mattered was the resonance that seeing them prompted in those who deciphered them on the basis of their own previous experience. (Chicago and London: University of Chicago Press, 1994).

And now the written word has joined the world of broadcast. The mass media of television and radio have given us instantaneous transmission of images and sound, vastly shrinking our world and just as vastly increasing our understanding of it. For the first time, the Internet gives us a mass medium for the instantaneous transmission of text. Not only that, it's a mass medium controllable by an individual. With it, a person's words can travel not just to one person via print or fax, not just to a group of people through the intercession of a government, corporation, or publisher, but to anyone on the planet who chooses to search for them. Now individuals, geniuses and crackpots alike, have joined the ranks of the bureaucrats and the pointy-haired managers with their ability to transmit the written word to the masses.

Visualizing Discourse

To further quote Henri-Jean Martin in *The History and Power of Writing*, "writing exists only by right of previous speech, thought or spoken, and its first aim is to set down spoken discourse in visual form." Well that seems fair enough; we can't write or speak until we think, even though there's some evidence to suggest the contrary.

But is writing a transforming act? In the same book, Martin says the following about writing:

> It is not revolutionary but appears every time that a revolution in communications and exchanges prompts

a fusion into a larger whole. Where this occurs it accelerates the changes set in motion within the society. There are two reasons for this. The first is that culture is nothing but what the thought of successive generations has produced; it permits the storage of that thought. The second is that writing casts speech onto a two-dimensional space and fixes it there, thus permitting speech to be an object of reflection outside of any context. Furthermore, because it visualizes discourse, writing prompts new sorts of connections in the reasoning process.

There's no question that a revolution in communications has been going on for a good part of the century and now we've added to it the ability to instantly transmit stored thought, the opportunity to reflect upon that stored thought, and the ability to create unlimited connections between it all. And those abilities and opportunities now belong to individuals, not just to governments or corporations.

To help figure out what this will do to the way we communicate, let's take a look at what our relationship has been with the written word in the past and how it has affected us.

A CHANGING RELATIONSHIP WITH TEXT

Mesopotamia dot COM

You wouldn't think that accountants would be at the vanguard of literary evolution, but they are to blame for the invention of the written word. In fact, most advances in literacy and mathematics are spurred by commerce. It was the Mesopotamian bean-counters, not the poets, who established cuneiform as the first written language. They inscribed pictures and counts of objects bought and sold (in sections called calculi using a base 60 number system) so that there would be no cheating on deals between people in distant cities. ("You owe me 40 oxen, not 20, and I have the tablets to prove it!") Writing was the first form of creating a presence in a distant place; it was also a means to register transactions and manage the accumulation of wealth. And during the Renaissance, most of the huge volume of correspondence of the time was devoted to a similar management of distant commercial exchanges.

The written word has appeared in many different forms and each form has flavored our relationship with the text. When ancient Romans used to scroll through words, they unrolled a physical scroll made of papyrus pages pasted together. They would read a page (with words in two columns, no spaces between the words) and then unroll the next page, while at the same time rolling up the previous page. Since the average scroll was about 10 yards long, skipping from the last page of the scroll to the first involved a lot more work than it does to skip pages in today's books. But the scroll was a big improvement over engraving words into clay tablets. It wasn't until the third or fourth century that people started writing on both sides of the parchment, piling the pages on top of one other and binding them into what we now think of as a book.

And of course the medium made a difference, as well as the exchanges it generated. You can encode information much faster on papyrus than you can in stone. Once papyrus appeared as the medium of choice, scrolls became standardized and their numbers skyrocketed, with the library in Alexandria containing over a half million. Likewise, indexes and tables of contents didn't appear until books were bound and you could flip through the pages rather than rolling through a scroll; there's not much point in an index or table of contents if it takes you 20 minutes to get to the right page. Likewise, the invention of paper and movable type in Europe set off a great boom, with print shops springing up everywhere, run by renaissance yuppies looking to make a buck and creating in the process a marketplace in which ideas could be bought and sold. Those ideas then proceeded to shape the course of history.

The Solitary Reader

Initially, scrolls or books weren't read as we know it today. Readers spoke the written word aloud to a group, using the text as a script, much like talking heads on television use a teleprompter. "Thus for some time no one imagined that discourse could be cast in any other language, or follow any other rhetoric, than that of the spoken word," says Martin. Even though people wrote words, they were used as an aid to memory in what was clearly still an oral tradition.

It wasn't until well into the Middle Ages that reading was even thought of as a solitary affair. "Henceforth the reader looked at a page rather than listening to a text, and his eyes moved over the two dimensional surface seeking a particular word or scanning for reference points or colored letters. By the same token, any reasoned argument . . . took on an objective existence," says Martin. The tradition of a single individual curling up with a book was thus born with the medieval creation of a one-on-one communication between a writer and a solitary reader; the speaker turned into an author, at once more personal yet more removed. Back then, if someone disagreed with something you were reading out loud, they had the physical proximity to slap the daylights out of you. The read manuscript put an end to that for the most part; if someone wanted to smack you around for something you wrote they would have to track you down.

But the read manuscript did offer a way to react, since to acquire a book before the invention of printing, you had to copy it yourself or pay someone to copy it. This gave scribes the opportunity to add their own embellishments to the text, including notations, commentary, and the frequent addition or correction. As a result, the manuscript not only contained text that changed over time, it contained rubrics (i.e., additions to the text in red ink that outlined the structure and helped explain the material) and lengthy commentaries. Each time a manuscript was copied, it gained a bit more embellishment and annotation, as each scribe added something to the work.

The Logic of the Book

The printed book also created its own relationship with text. Books were first printed exactly as duplicates of manuscripts, complete with rubrics, commentary, and hand-painted decoration. Over time, however, these embellishments disappeared, leaving only the undecorated text, alone on the page with ever-shrinking margins. Books became pruned and standardized, the result of being a manufactured object. The mechanics of printing also inhibited the placing of words and pictures together on a page, so printed books lost the hand-copied manuscript's integration of text and image. As a result, images were herded together away from the relevant text; sometimes they were even printed as entirely separate volumes. "Thus the Enlightenment marked the moment of triumph of the text over the image, of a certain form of typographical rhetoric over the rhetoric of the spoken word, and of the serially produced object," says Martin.

Very briefly, we can see some common impulses in our use of the written word. First, there's the obvious desire to visualize discourse: to set something down and integrate it with image and decoration. Then, once it's stored and reflected upon, we see the impulse to comment upon it, either by way of clarification, elaboration, or commentary. Finally there's the desire to create a complex structure of information or thought that stands by itself and can be communicated as a whole from author to reader and from which connections can be drawn.

FILES OF WORDS

THE FLAVOR OF TEXT ON THE INTERNET

When we think of text on the Internet, the fact that it's transmitted electronically is of course important, but that is not the only thing happening. The human impulse to visualize discourse, to create a complex structure of thought and image, to rant after reflection (or more often before), and to make connections, now has a new place to flower.

While not as intimate as a book (I've yet to take my beloved iMac to bed with me), a Web site offers a place of almost infinite space and complexity for the storage of information and thought, accessible to anyone who chooses to go to it. And just as in the past, when the level of complexity of the stored thought reached a certain level, the need for rubrication (i.e., additions to the text that outlined the structure and helped explain the material) kicked in. We don't use red ink for that any more, but we do have a fairly clear set of rubrics for helping people navigate the huge amounts of text and image found in Web sites, including clickable tables of contents and indexes, next/previous navigation buttons, search features, and clickable external references and bibliographies.

Two other impulses that appeared in the medieval manuscript have also surfaced on the Web. One is the embellishment of words made possible by being a single entity. A Web site, unlike a book, is not a mass-produced item but a one-of-a-kind creation, even though it might be mirrored on multiple sites. A Web site is handcrafted for the most part so it can be elaborated over time like a physical manuscript. And as the site evolves, the visitor always gets the most recent additions. The other is the fact that words and pictures are easily interwoven once again. More than just eye candy, the integration of text and image offers new possibilities for visual forms of communication.

Finally, commentary has returned in full force, even though

it's no longer transcribed in the margins of a manuscript. The number, quality and size of the Web sites that have blossomed in the past few years is incredible, as is the amount of reaction these sites have generated. Any topic of any consequence at all has a huge number of discussion groups associated with it, with endless diatribes back and forth, some of which are actually useful. And with email, an author is once again an easy target for flak.

Hypertext – Connection Made Manifest

The Internet offers an outlet for many impulses that we've seen implemented in written media of the past. It also offers one key feature that hasn't been realized before: *hypertext*. Hypertext is the mechanism you use when you click on a Web page link to see a new Web page. Hypertext provides a way to make the connection between related pages physical by linking words or images to another file. When you put your cursor over linked words or images, it turns into a finger; you click and you see the linked page. It is a wonderfully efficient way to connect one idea to another, regardless of where or how that idea is represented.

In the past, sequence and proximity were the only ways to relate groups of words. Paragraphs followed one another in chapters and chapters followed one another in books; related books were issued in sets. Now, by the way that we write our hypertext links, we have the ability to connect groups of words directly within a work (e.g., paragraphs, sections, chapters, glossaries, bibliographies, notes). We also have the ability to link pages externally to other pages, creating complex repositories of thought spanning the globe.

The architecture of hypertext allows an excellent structuring of knowledge because it puts the connection right where you need it. For example, if you define a concept in a book and then use it more than once, you must either define the concept again or refer to the previous definition's specific location. Being able to link directly to the definition from each usage is clearly a more useful way to communicate.

Hypertext also allows us to create dynamic webs of connection. While the set of links in one Web site may be created by a single person, the links available at the next linked site would be created by someone else. A person following a thread of links through various sites is therefore taking a path through information that no one person or organization can design or control.

Breaking Down Barriers

Text and hypertext on the Internet is the capstone of the communications revolution of the past century since it not only offers a medium for the mass, instant transmission of text, it also puts that medium in the hands of the individual. The Internet turbocharges the power of the word, which is awesome enough to begin with; it accelerates the breakdown of barriers and expands the context in which we see each other. Villages in the past were small, self-contained and compartmentalized. Today, our villages and neighborhoods may still be small but they are definitely not self-contained or compartmentalized. Rather, they are intertwined in a great link of commerce, culture, and information. The power of the Internet is the power of the word – the power each individual now has to create complex repositories of thought and to enter into a conversation on that thought with anyone else on the planet.

What We Were After All Along?

It is still quite mind-boggling to me (if not to my children) to be able to get words delivered via the Internet to my computer from millions of different Web sites all over the planet in a matter of seconds. It is even more mind-boggling to have my words read and responded to by people all over the world, even if those people may be few in number. Words used to be stuck to paper; if you wanted the word you had to have the paper too. Now words have been freed, morphing into an electronic form where digital copies exist in files going from servers to clients, displayed on a computer monitor until the next link is clicked. Given the explosion of words on the Web and the various desires to visualize discourse that the Web satisfies, I can't help but wonder if the Internet is a form of communication that we've been after from the very beginning. Digitized words will never replace words in books, but they make a mighty companion.

To close, here's one final thought of Henri-Jean Martin's from *The History and Power of Writing*:

> On every occasion, oral communication (and communication by images) has developed along with writing in a world of expanding cities and accelerating exchanges. And now, in the last few decades, a society of simultaneity has come to be organized, as if it were a logical point of arrival.

And this he wrote before the blooming of the Internet!

Files of Pictures

**If I could tell the story in words,
I wouldn't need to lug a camera.**

– Lewis Hine

JUST LIKE we send files of words, we can send files of pictures across the Internet from servers to clients. It's easy to see how words can be digitized in files; we represent each character by a unique set of bits and just string them together one after another, along with the necessary framing information. But how do we turn pictures into bits – into files of 0s and 1s?

These are the common ways:

- Scan a picture. The scanner creates an image file on disk.
- When you get your pictures developed, order a photo CD. Each image file on the CD contains one picture.
- Use a digital camera to take pictures and download the image files to disk.
- Use a graphics program to draw images yourself or fiddle with already existing digitized images and save them to disk.
- Use video capture software to save a digitized video image to disk.

Once an image is digitized in a Web-friendly file format, it sits on a Web server awaiting the click that will cause it to see the light of day. There are a number of different image file formats; one popular graphics program lists 114 formats. But they all share some common digitizing strategies.

Image File Guts - Pictures as 0s and 1s

We create colors with light by mixing, as we do with paint, only the primary colors are different and the light is projected rather than reflected.

Using an RGB (Red, Green, Blue) color mixing scheme, a monitor makes colors by squirting specific amounts of red, green, and blue light onto each *pixel* (i.e., dot on the screen) that is needed to form a picture. Image files tell the monitor, or the printer if you're printing, how to squirt those colors.

We digitize image files in one of two ways: with *bit maps* or with *vectors*. Bit-mapped image files encode pictures by describing each dot in the picture as some combination of colors; vector images use mathematical formulas to describe the paths taken by the shapes of the objects in the picture as well as their colors. Vector images have many advantages. They are often small in size and scalable; you can magnify them by zooming and actually see more detail at the higher magnification. If you zoom a bit-mapped image, on the other hand, all you get is bigger dots. While work is progressing on standards for vector graphics on the Web, they are not yet widely used. Most of the images found on the Web today are bit-mapped images.

A bit-mapped image file uses 0s and 1s to store directions for squirting colors into each pixel needed to display the image. In order to display a nice teal green, the file might tell your monitor to squirt the pixel with no red, green at 40% intensity, and blue at 40% intensity. Since the file has to describe each pixel, the bigger the image, the bigger the file. Here's an example. Let's say you had an image that was six inches by six inches.

- At 72 dots to the inch, a typical monitor resolution, you'd need (72 dots times 6 inches)^2 or 186,624 separate sets of pixel-squirting directions.
- If each set of pixel-squirting directions took up 8 bits, typical for image files on the Web, you would need up to a 186K file to store that one 6 x 6 image.
- If each set of pixel-squirting directions took up 32 bits (needed for a realistic photo image), the file would be upwards of 700K.

A word file of that same size could easily hold an entire novel. It takes a lot more 0s and 1s to represent pictures than it does to represent words.

Fortunately, *compression* is the other common digitizing strategy that image files employ. One common compression technique takes neighboring pixels that look the same and encodes them as a block rather than as individual pixels; another technique takes the colors the human eye can't distinguish and gets rid of them. Nevertheless, image files in general are quite large and consequently take some time to move across the Web.

Pictures are Cool

Given the complexity of digitized images and the network resources they eat up, why do we bother? Well, because pictures are cool. The Internet was originally conceived as a means to transmit text; it existed in that state for years, used by research scientists but mostly unknown to the rest of us. Then, in 1990, Tim Berners-Lee (www.w3.org/People/Berners-Lee-Bio.html/) created the World Wide Web by conceiving and publishing its underlying protocols and standards (HTTP, URL, and HTML) and developing an initial software implementation. That gave the Internet both hypertext and images (images if you happened to surf using a NeXT machine). Then in 1993, Marc Andreessen and others at University of Illinois NSCA wrote a browser called Mosaic, which Andreessen later redeveloped as Netscape. This was the first browser written for Mac and Windows as well as UNIX and was the first to display images within a page rather than in a separate window. There was some concern at the time that graphics on the Web would clog up the Internet; that pictures of Klingons and other visual frivolities would use up network resources that had been previously devoted to the transmittal of serious, scholarly research papers. But as NSCA's John Mittelhauser said, "the concept of adding in an image just for the sake of adding an image . . . made sense because face it, they made pages look cool."

The coolness of pictures enabled the "dot com" commercial exchanges that drove the explosive growth of the Web because without them no one would buy online. And it provided a vehicle for a visual means of communication that is different from, but complementary to, communication via the written word.

Visual Knowledge

In *The History and Power of Writing*, Henri-Jean Martin says that thought precedes speech or writing. Steven Pinker in *The Language Instinct* says something similar:

> The idea that thought is the same as language is an example of what can be called a conventional absurdity. . . . Sometimes it is not easy to find any words that properly convey a thought. When we hear or read, we usually remember the gist, not the exact words, so there has to be such a thing as a gist that is not the same as a bunch of words. (New York: William Morrow and Company, Inc., 1994).

Images are the other thing that we use, besides words, to communicate the gist of our thoughts as well as the gist of the complex mounds of information through which we daily navigate.

FILES OF PICTURES

Edward Tufte has written three gorgeous books on information design, explaining how to use pictures to convey the gist of complex information. He describes his books as follows:

- *The Visual Display of Quantitative Information* - pictures as numbers
- *Envisioning Information* - pictures as nouns
- *Visual Explanations* - pictures as verbs

In them he explores how best to use a two-dimensional space to convey the meaning of the objects and events around us and how, often more importantly, to uncover that meaning by being able to visualize all the pieces of the puzzle in the right relationship at the right time. Images are key to this visualization and are essential to the communication of certain kinds of meaning. For example, any design methodology that handles a high level of complexity always ends up with a pictorial component (e.g., graphical software design tools, CAD/CAM, blueprints, schematics). There is a way of conveying complex information that can only be fully done pictorially.

Images can also take us where the human eye cannot go, from pictures of galaxies to images in an electron microscope, and from images that slow down time to images that speed it up.

Photographs

Images are also powerful instruments of social change. Lewis Hine, whose quote opens this chapter, was a documentary photographer famous for his images of immigrant housing and working conditions in the United States in the early 1900s. He is especially noted for his work with the National Child Labor Committee. Hine believed in the power of his medium to persuade; his work was instrumental in the eventual enactment of child labor and safety laws. If he were still alive, he would undoubtedly have a magnificent Web site. In fact his pictures, along with a vast array of other old photographs, populate numerous Web sites today. Images on the Web can therefore convey information not only about what the world is like now, but also about how it used to be.

Images can also speak directly to our intuition. In her book *On Photography*, Susan Sontag says:

> The ultimate wisdom of the photographic image is to say: 'This is the surface. Now think—or rather feel, intuit—what is beyond it, what the reality must be like if it looks this way.' Photographs, which cannot themselves explain anything, are inexhaustible invitations to deduction, speculation, and fantasy. (New York: Dell Publishing Company, 1977).

Pictures speak a language that everyone understands. The beauty of the Web is that it easily integrates image and word and leverages the power of both. In his book *Envisioning Information*, Edward Tufte says that it is a natural combination, much like speech and gesture: "To envision information—and what bright and splendid visions can result—is to work at the intersection of images, word, number, art." (Cheshire, Connecticut: Graphics Press, 1990).

Art

The Web is swimming with images, including ad banners, buttons, logos, photos of people and places, technical documents, 360-degree zoomable graphics, reproductions of art, and dancing hamsters (www.hamsterdance.com). What we haven't seen much of is Web-native art (except maybe the dancing hamsters). Images displayed on monitors are luminous, lit from behind like stained glass windows; they have great potential as a medium of their own for visual art alongside the more traditional media. English art critic Sr. Wendy Beckett said in her Bill Moyers interview that "art is a communication of personal truth – the artist's personal truth confronting your personal truth – what you're meant to be but maybe haven't yet become." I can't help but wonder what art forms will bloom on the Web, taking advantage of its luminosity as well as motion and sound. And I can't help but wonder in what manner such art will enrich the people who view it.

With the evolution of the Web, the Internet offers us a medium for the mass, instant transmission not only of text but of image and art. And it puts that medium in the hands of the individual. It also lets each one of us turn into radio and video broadcasters.

Files of
Sound and Motion

WE'VE SEEN how to turn 0s and 1s into words and pictures. Now let's see how those lovely, elemental bits can be used to encode Mozart, a radio program, or a video.

Sound as 0s and 1s

Digitized sound made its first public appearance with the adoption of the CD and compact disk player as the audio lover's tool of choice. The Internet has given digitized sound a second wind with new audio standards and audio client and server software, prompting the blossoming of sound files all over the Web.

There are a number of different ways to digitize sound. On a CD, it's done by looking at the structure of the electrical signal from a recording microphone 44,100 times every second and creating a digital trace of that structure in separate, sequential chunks of 16 bits (2 bytes) for each 44,100th of a second of sound. When the sound is reproduced, the shape of the electrical signal to the speakers is formed based upon those stored numbers.

CD sound files are big because the signal is sampled so frequently (44,100 times a second), because of the extent of data stored in each sampling (16 bits or 2 bytes), because two chan-

FILES OF SOUND AND MOTION

nels are sampled to create stereo sound, and because the files are uncompressed. To store an hour of sound on a CD, you would need at least the following amount of space:

- ❐ 44,100 chunks a second x 2 bytes = 88,200 bytes or about 88 Kilobytes for a second of mono sound
- ❐ times 60 times 2 or about 10+ Megabytes for a minute of stereo sound
- ❐ times 60 or about 635 Megabytes for an hour of stereo sound

Digitized sound takes up a lot of space. You could pack about 600 novels into the space it takes to hold an hour of music; that's a big file. And size matters, especially on the Web, where size is a determinant of download time and where nobody likes to wait. But ever-resourceful software developers have figured out how to whack that size down by compressing the file. They also figured out a way to start playing the file before the whole thing downloads, a technique called *streaming*. But whether the bits are on a CD or in a file on the Web, the idea is the same – the bits control the shape of the electrical signal to the speakers. And now you can get the bits not only on your CD but in files on the Web.

If you want to see how this works, get on the Web and download some client software that plays Web audio files. A good place to start is www.real.com for RealPlayer. Alternatively, you could go to your search engine of choice and do a search on "web audio player" or "web audio client" and see what pops up.

Streaming Audio

Each audio file has a URL and downloads as a result of a click on a link. Then the player (i.e., client) launches and begins to play the file. If you have to wait for the entire file to download before the player starts to play, however, you might be waiting a long time due to the large size of most audio files.

To solve the problem of long downloads, in the mid-1990s a company called Progressive Networks (now called RealNetworks) invented streaming audio. In a streaming audio file, after you click on a link and the audio file starts to download, the software is smart enough to do a number of things at once. It starts to play the beginning of the file and it continues to manage the download of the rest of the file. Furthermore, it hangs on to just enough of the file so that if the download is temporarily interrupted, it can continue to send a smooth stream of bits to the hardware that creates the sound in the speakers. As a result, the generated sound usually remains smooth despite network traffic.

RealNetworks' client software is called RealAudio (now RealPlayer). To play a RealAudio file, you would need the RealPlayer client and you would also need to find a file served with Real server software, since the server and the client talk to one another to manage the streaming of the file. The Web is filled with RealAudio files. These files might have URLs that look something like this:

> http://www.weloveourselves.com/themesong.ra
> http://www.mozartrules.com/piano/sonatas/k545.ra
> http://www.thegoodolddayz.com/itsiebitsiespider.ra

With a server, a client, and a file with a URL, you have the three things you need to create a communication on the Web, which in this case is the communication of sound from one who serves it up to one who listens to it.

MP3

There are other flavors of streaming audio on the Web, the most interesting being a sound file format called MP3. MP3 is a popular standard for two reasons. First, its file sizes are much smaller than CD file sizes – about ten times smaller – yet it produces excellent sound. Second, it is an open standard (more on this in the chapter on Open Standards). A typical site serving MP3 sound files offers hundreds or thousands of individual sound files filled with music categorized by genre. Usually the downloads are free even though they are often accompanied by a "purchase opportunity." You might sample a track or two and then decide to buy the related CD. These sites are a great way for lesser-known artists to popularize their work and for better-known artists to tantalize by giving the world an audio peek at a new release. They are typically high-traffic sites generating revenue streams from ads and purchases. To see what's currently out there, get on the Web and try a search on "MP3." Many catalogs and search engines now also have huge sections devoted solely to MP3.

At the other end, you need a client that plays MP3 files. Since it is an open standard, most audio and video clients (e.g., RealPlayer, QuickTime) now can play MP3 files as well as the files for which they were originally designed. But a new class of client software has appeared specifically for playing just MP3 files. Such clients create what looks like a snazzy CD player on your monitor, complete with buttons, controls, and displays. The player also lets you create play lists which select, sequence, and store the audio files (i.e., songs). Play lists function much like bookmarks in a browser, remembering the location of each file and letting you get to it with ease.

These MP3 clients are usually offered as *shareware* or *freeware* downloads. If it's shareware, you download the client, try it out, and purchase it if you keep it. If it's freeware, you download a "lite" version for free with the hope that you will like it enough to come back later and purchase the full-featured version. To find one, try a search on "MP3 player."

Since sound can live in bits, since MP3 is an open standard, and since software developers are quite clever, they've figured out how to copy the bit stream from an audio CD and reformat it into the much more compact MP3 format. With *CD ripper* software, you can convert your favorite audio CD tracks into much smaller MP3 files, store them in play lists, and play them from your hard disk or home speakers. You can also enhance your playlists with searchable data you can download from the Internet, including the CD name, artist, track title, track timing, and genre. CD ripper software also gives you the opportunity, and some argue the right, to serve MP3 files yourself or share them with your friends, creating a huge copyright conundrum.

We can download and serve sound files and play them to our heart's content. But what's in them? Mostly music, some silliness (e.g., the sound of a cartoon character burping), the occasional telephone conversation, and radio.

Internet Radio

Like any communication, radio works on the common model of:

>Sender - the radio broadcast
>Signal - radio waves
>Receiver - the radio

If we can digitize a song we can digitize a radio program; the bits don't know the difference. So now we have:

>Sender - the radio broadcast server
>Signal - streaming audio file
>Receiver - client audio player

That's great, but what's the point? Why not just turn on the radio? Besides being cool, radio over the Internet solves a transmission problem. To hear a normal radio broadcast, you have to be within range of the station. If the broadcast is to carry beyond the range of a single broadcast transmitter, a broadcast network is required. But with radio on the Internet, you can be anyplace on the planet and still receive it – the Internet becomes the broad-

FILES OF SOUND AND MOTION

cast network. Want to listen to the nightly news from Moscow? How about Irish talk radio? Rock and roll from Australia? Just find the right URL and you're in business.

What has to happen for you to get radio over the Internet? First of all, someone has to serve it. Someone has to digitize a radio broadcast and put it on a server on the Web. For example, a radio station might choose to digitize its evening news or its afternoon talk program. Each day, or each hour, it would digitize a new file and put it on the server using a consistent URL so people could find it. Alternatively, a radio station might digitize a live feed, streaming the audio as the broadcast is made. Both have advantages. Live broadcasts (i.e., *webcasts*) are obviously timely; you get them as they occur. A stored broadcast, on the other hand, sits on the server for a certain amount of time (e.g., until it is updated) and can be accessed whenever you choose. This is variously called *audio on demand* or *pointcasting*; it is content going to an audience of one, when you decide to listen. Furthermore, since the entire broadcast is available on the server, you can fast-forward or replay segments just as you do with video on a VCR. If your favorite Hawaiian radio show is on in the middle of the night, you can get it the next morning and enjoy the parts you want to hear at your leisure.

Once the file is served, you have to click on the link to get the file. Finally, you would need the right client to play the audio file and listen to the program.

The URLs for streaming audio files might look like this:

> www.lilyradio.com/nightlynews.ra
> www.lilyradio.com/live.ra

That's how you can use the Web to listen to radio stations all over the world that have digitized their broadcasts. And you can not only listen, you can be a broadcaster yourself.

GETTING THE WEB

Broadcasting Internet Radio

Existing radio stations have paid millions of dollars for their broadcast licenses. Typically, they serve some broadcasts on the Internet as well to take advantage of the new medium. This practice is fondly referred to as *shovelware* – the dumping of existing content onto a new medium. However, anyone with the inclination and the software can be a broadcaster simply by digitizing and serving audio files; you don't have to be a traditional radio broadcaster first. And more importantly, you don't need to pay for the multimillion dollar radio license since you're not twiddling waves on the scarce radio broadcast band, you're twiddling bits on a Web server. The mass medium of radio broadcasting is now in the hands of the individual.

Radio broadcasts over the Web also transcend national boundaries. Since the Web is its own broadcast network and nobody owns the Web, nobody controls what gets served. Normal radio (and TV) programs are still broadcast locally via cable or broadcast towers so most of what we get comes from within national boundaries. If we get a show from another country, it's because a network or a cable company has picked it up. In the United States we see BBC offerings from Great Britain that have been selected for us, typically by PBS. While we might be able to pick up BBC World News or ITN on a local channel, we probably don't have access to Irish talk shows or the nightly news from Russia.

For radio and TV, access to such broadcasts is up to the network and cable programmers that serve your broadcast area. For Internet radio, access is up to two parties and two parties alone:

- The broadcaster, who digitizes the audio and places it on a server in a common Web audio format.
- The listener, who finds the audio program, downloads the file, and has the proper client to play the file.

FILES OF SOUND AND MOTION

With global access, you can be a network programmer:

- You can digitize and stream audio.
- You can use various clients and servers created through open standards.
- You can listen to music or radio from anywhere on the planet.
- You can broadcast music or radio all over the planet.

And you can do the same thing for video.

Video on the Web

As a result of compression and streaming technology as well as open standards, audio on the Web has hit that magic point where growth is self-generating. Cool clients and good servers cause the creation of more content, which generates improvements in clients and servers and the creation of even more content, spreading music and radio all over the Web. The story isn't quite the same yet for video.

Video files, even when they are compressed, are huge. An MP3 audio file might need about 120 Megabytes to hold two hours of music; a digital video file on a DVD might need about 5 Gigabytes to hold a two-hour movie. That's 120 million vs. 5 billion – over 40 times as big. Even with compression, video files are much larger than audio files and still too big to download easily on the Web.

What can be done until we all have high-speed, broadband connections to the Internet? Three things:

- Make a smaller picture.
- Stream it.
- Compress until it hurts.

The footprint of a typical Web video is small. Rather than filling the screen like a DVD movie, it only fills a box approximately one and a half by two inches. And the video is streamed just like audio is streamed. The RealPlayer client and the QuickTime 4 client as well as the Microsoft player now stream video as well as audio, allowing you to see the beginning of a video clip while the rest continues to download. Finally, the compression done during the streaming is quite severe, generating a fairly jumpy and mushy image compared to what you might see on a multimedia CD.

When striking a balance between making files small by throwing away data in the video stream and keeping a quality image, streaming compression designers have tilted toward smaller files at the expense of quality. See for yourself. Download the current streaming video player from RealNetworks, Apple, or Microsoft and look at some video. The resolution of the video remaining after streaming and compression is adequate but not great. However, it enables access to video served worldwide and that's what counts. Along with listening to the nightly news from Moscow on the radio, you can see it on video, complete with spinning logos, news clips and talking Russian heads. You can watch debates live from Great Britain's House of Commons; in October, if you tune in the Good Morning program from New Zealand, you can hear the hosts discussing New Zealand's lovely spring. You can watch the news from South Korea or India or Iran; you can view music videos from just about anywhere and see just about anything that someone has chosen to serve. Even if you don't understand the language you'll understand the pictures. You can also be a broadcaster, serving your own video to whomever wants to watch.

The limiting factor today for video on the Web is bandwidth, which we will explore further in a later chapter. As that increases with the roll out of high-speed, broadband Internet connections, quality will increase and video will proliferate, just like MP3. And anyone who wants can get into the game.

Files of Logic

SO FAR WE'VE seen files containing words, pictures, sound and motion go from servers to clients, opening up all kinds of possibilities for communication and exchange. In all cases, the file contains a digital representation of words, pictures, sound and motion and the client translates that digital representation into something we can see and hear, displaying the contents of the file on the monitor or playing it through the speakers.

Now let's stop for a minute and think of what is going on in the computer, since you use a computer to surf and computers work by enabling software programs to transform inputs into outputs.

Your word processor is a software program that takes the words you enter and creates an output that is a word processing document. Your spreadsheet is a software program that takes the numbers you enter and creates an output that is a spreadsheet document. Likewise, your browser is a software program that takes a file as input from a server and displays it as output on your monitor. And if we were to describe the basic functionality of email, chat, instant messaging, and news group clients and servers, it would be to send our words to others and receive their words in return. You could say that most of the traffic on the

Internet is a result of software programs sending words, pictures, sound, and motion back and forth and displaying or playing them when they arrive.

ð

We use software programs on computers *not* connected to the Internet for widely diverse jobs. We use them to control air traffic, to launch satellites, to run the stock market, to print books, to account for revenues, expenses, assets and liabilities, to buy and sell, to manage inventory, to design machines, to make movies, and most anything else that goes on in society today.

But so far, with software programs on computers connected to the Internet, we're mostly sending words, pictures, sound, and motion back and forth. On the Internet, we're still doing "show and tell." What happens when we start creating Web clients and servers that not only do show and tell, but do the million other things that software is known for? Let's start by seeing what can happen when individuals can not only surf Web sites, but talk back to the Web site server.

Smart Servers

Back when Marc Andreessen and others were writing the Mosaic browser at University of Illinois NSCA, another NSCA team was working on the server software. While they were at it, they developed a clever standard called the Common Gateway Interface (CGI) which did two things:

- ❐ It allowed the server to pass along a message from a person visiting a site to the other programs running at the computer installation.
- ❐ It allowed the server to pass back to the visitor (via a Web page) a chunk of information from those other programs.

This gave a person visiting a Web site the ability to send messages to the site. Programs on the site's computers could process that message and send a customized Web page back to the visitor, all in the space of a few seconds. This process allows the contents of Web pages to be dynamically constructed by other software programs based on information or requests sent by each individual. It also provides a mechanism for a huge installed base of existing computer software to "get on the Web."

If you visit Amazon.com or any of the other electronic retailers on the Web, it's still mostly a browsing experience until you actually purchase something. Then, you have to tell the Web server a few things, like what you want to buy, who you are, and of course your credit card number. When you fill out the online form and click the "Purchase" button, you send the Web server a message containing all that information. The message goes to the server and then on to the mountain of software on the other side of the server that manages inventory, invoicing, collection, shipping and tracking, kicking off a flurry of activity that results in a charge to your credit card and a package on your doorstep a few days later.

Because of the Common Gateway Interface and its more recent descendants, servers have become quite intelligent. They tap into the wealth of logic that people and corporations use day in and day out, letting that logic provide the up-to-date information we see in Web sites when we check the weather forecast, get headlines and stock quotes, track the progress of a package, get the traffic report, or look up the arrival time of a commercial airline flight.

All the computers on the planet are filled with words and pictures itching to be shared. They are also filled with logic itching to process information. All this logic needs is a Web interface and people or organizations with information to process. At some point, most of the business now handled via the telephone in a very annoying manner ("Please listen to the following menu options that have been recently updated for your benefit bla bla bla ... Press one to ...") will one day be handled via a Web interface that could be clicked through and finished in the time it would take to listen to the "recently updated menu options." All those telephone interfaces are stepping stones to a Web interface between you and someone else's computer system. They arise to solve a need to provide or receive information that is high volume and repetitive. Eventually we'll be manipulating our own digital records. We'll transact business directly with various corporate databases rather than talking to poor humans crazed with boredom who type information into computers and tell us what the computer says. If I can swipe my debit card at the grocery store and have the amount deducted from my checking account, I ought to be able to enter that same debit card number at the various Web sites of the companies that send me monthly bills. If the information being transferred is not vast, if the connection is secure, and if the business rules of the transaction can be rendered in logic, it can happen on the Web in a pleasing and efficient manner.

Amazon.com is an example of how this kind of interaction can work. When I visit, besides handling my purchase, the Amazon server greets me by name and presents a list of books that might be of interest based upon my past purchases. Some recommendations are loopy but some are on the mark and the idea is intriguing even if it is carried out by a computer. The Amazon server also tells me what books are of interest to other groups of readers (e.g., people who live in Chicago). When I click on a particular book, I see professional reviews as well as reviews by actual individuals; I also see a list of related books purchased by people who also purchased this book. And once I enter it, Amazon remembers all the information relevant to my making a credit card purchase as well as remembering the names and addresses of people to whom I send books. From where I click, thanks to smart servers, the online retail experience is good.

Smart Servers - Business to Business

Online retailing is a popular example of smart servers at work, but it is just the beginning, representing a Web relationship between a company and its customers. We can also look forward to some mighty productivity gains when businesses work out Web relationships with their suppliers, using their computers to communicate directly with each other. E-business happens because it can, and it works; it creates a whole new level of enterprise and productivity. As an example, let's go back to Amazon.

Those millions of books at Amazon don't come out of thin air. The transactions through which a publisher lists books at Amazon is also completely Web-based. A publisher selling a book through Amazon can perform all the following functions online:

- Enroll as a book seller at Amazon.
- Receive book orders.
- Enhance how the book appears online.
- Promote the book online.
- Check current sales and availability.
- Receive automatic reorders.

Only two things in the process don't happen online. The publisher must ship the books to the Amazon warehouse and Amazon must send a check to the publisher.

This simple picture of a publisher's interaction with Amazon is a small model of the way businesses will interact with one another in the future. Known as *e-commerce* or *business-to-business (B2B)*, it is the way in which businesses will deal with suppliers, service providers, and other partners to create their products and services. And it all happens thanks to smart servers on the Web.

That's what can happen when server software gets smart. What happens when client software gets smart?

Smart Clients

Client software is already pretty smart and getting smarter. Your average browser now contains a veritable library of plug-ins and functionality to read email, browse news groups, transfer files, and play audio and video. And other clients are becoming correspondingly feature-rich. MP3 players, for example, are showing up with all kinds of snazzy visual interfaces complete with not only bass and treble knobs but graphic equalizers and slick play list manipulation.

And clients are getting smarter by doing new things. Sherlock, on the Macintosh, for example, will intelligently query a list of electronic retail sites for a specific product you suggest and not only find the product for you, but find it at the best price. So it not only searches, but searches and evaluates. Clients are evolving by getting better at filtering the vast and overwhelming amount of information on the Web to help you find what you need rather than finding thousands of irrelevant sites. So servers are getting smarter and clients are getting smarter. All this smartness is also filling up our hard disks with software.

Downloading Programs

If bits were money, we'd all be billionaires because we can download bits that in turn allow us to download an almost infinite number of *more* bits! This is an enabling complexity; once it reaches a certain level of evolution, a whole new thing bursts on the scene that grows out of, but is different than, what came before. Now we can have client software downloading not only files of words, pictures, sound and motion, but files that contain software. Why not? It's all just another set of bits. Want to try a new client? Just go to the Web site, download the file, run the install program and you have a new software client that allows you to access a whole new set of files from Internet servers. Want to try getting audio over the Web? Download the audio client and surf for sites that contain audio files you can download and play. How about video? Download the video client and surf for sites that contain video files you can download and play. Want to help search for extraterrestrial intelligence? Go to the SETI site, download the SETI client, and download a file to process with your new SETI client.

The Internet enables not only the publishing and broadcasting of words, pictures, sound and motion by individuals and organizations, it also enables the publishing of software. As we buy more software on the Web, more will be created and more people will go into the Web-based software development business. Most of the programs that you download (and pay for) on the Web today were developed, at least initially, by individuals or very small teams. The history of the Internet is filled with very creative people, not huge corporations, even though many of those initial software developments grew into corporations, leaving huge heaps of millionaires in their wakes. It could be an individual like you behind that next Wall Street Internet stock offering! According to the U. S. Census Bureau, the leading revenue generators (based on 1997 data) in the publishing sector were software publishers, followed by newspapers, then periodicals, and then book publishers. So, counter-intuitive as it might seem, there's money in logic!

The Telephone Company for Computers

Well that's the *what* of the Web: files of bits representing words, pictures, sound, motion, and logic, moving back and forth between servers and clients at the click of a link.

With the Web, individuals and organizations all over the planet now have:

- The power to publish and read complex repositories of thought and to enter into a dialog on that thought.
- The power to publish and view visual representations of knowledge, image and art.
- The power to broadcast or receive music, radio and video from anywhere at any time.
- The power to publish and access software and to create and utilize direct Web relationships with individuals and organizations anywhere at any time.

Not a bad way to launch the millennium!

۶۰

The Internet as we know it today is emerging from its infancy but its shape is still very much determined by its parents, the telephone network and the computer.

Part II

In Part II we think about why the Internet is the way it is – how computers and telephone networks shape the nature of the Internet.

GETTING THE WEB

Open Standards

THE TELEPHONE network is well over 100 years old. Computers have been around for more than 40 years and have been on the desktop for more than 20 years. Yet only since the mid-1990s have they propagated in a big way, giving life to the Internet and the Web.

What was the essential ingredient that made it happen and made it happen so fast? Good pedigree. Both the telephone industry and the computer industry are almost completely standards-driven.

Standards and Communication

Files of words, pictures, sound, motion, and logic generate a considerable amount of traffic on the Internet in their travels from servers to clients. That's a lot of 0s and 1s – hundreds of billions a second, give or take a few billion. How do we decipher all those 0s and 1s? How do we tell the bits that represent a Mozart sonata from the bits that represent a picture from the bits that represent a definition from the Oxford English Dictionary? With standards.

By using standards, we are able to turn billions of 0s and 1s into complex files of words, pictures, sound, motion, and logic that actually mean something. Standards provide the language that give context and therefore meaning to our 0s and 1s.

The Internet, like all communication, uses the model of the sender, the signal, and the receiver:

- Sender – the Server
- Signal – the File
- Receiver – the Client

For communication to take place, the sender and the receiver must understand the meaning of the signal. On the Internet and the Web, standards give meaning at many different levels to the bits flying back and forth in files between clients and servers. There are a huge number of standards that work with one another, layer upon layer, to enable just about any activity you could imagine on the Internet, from the most basic electrical interaction to high-level programming. In this chapter, we'll look at a small but crucial set – standards for files. We create meaning by agreeing upon standards for our files. They are the fertile soil in which client and server applications can grow, enabling new forms of communication and exchange.

The meaning of a file is given in two ways: first, by the type of file, and second by the standard that describes that file.

File Types

The MIME type (Multipurpose Internet Mail Extension) defines the type of file (e.g., Web page file, RealAudio audio file, QuickTime video file, etc.) that goes from the server to the client. Its peculiar name results from the fact that in the early days, email was the dominant file type on the Internet, so everything that came after it was considered an extension. The Internet Society (www.isoc.org) has defined hundreds of different MIME file types and each file on the Internet contains a MIME type identification. Your browser looks at that identification and then figures out how to display or play the file.

OPEN STANDARDS

File Standards

Once the browser knows the type of file, it can interpret it correctly based upon the standard that defines the structure of the file. When you write a Web page, you follow the standard called HTML (Hyper Text Markup Language). HTML allows you to mark up text to control its display in a browser. For example, if you want some words to show up in bold text, you put the characters `<B>` and `</B>` before and after the text you want in bold. If you follow the HTML standard when writing Web pages, anyone with a browser that supports the standard can view the Web pages you write.

Standards and the Birth of the Web

In 1990, Tim Berners-Lee wrote three standards (HTML, HTTP, URL) to implement a way to display, link, and find documents on any computer hooked to the Internet. By writing these three standards as well as the first browser, Tim Berners-Lee, with a little help from his friends, invented the World Wide Web. People saw what he had done, thought it was cool, and started writing Web pages of their own. Other folks like Marc Andreessen started writing better browsers and the Web grew like wildfire. Luckily for us, the standards that Berners-Lee wrote were open standards that anyone could use. And they were also robust enough to scale from a World Wide Web of a few files on a server in Switzerland to the hundreds of millions of files we have on the Web today. Tim Berners-Lee tells his story and relates his hopes for the future of his brainchild in his book *Weaving the Web: The Original Design and Ultimate Destiny of the World Wide Web by Its Inventor* (New York: HarperCollins Publishers, 1999). He went on to found the World Wide Web Consortium (www.w3.org), a group whose mission is to realize the full potential of the Web, primarily through the evolution of open standards.

Standards Today

Once someone thinks up a standard that catches on, it typically evolves through use and through formalization by a standards committee. There are thousands of people in the telecommunications and computer industries involved in debating and formalizing the various standards in use today. Many of these are Internet and Web standards or are used in the infrastructure of the network itself. Key standards organizations include the Internet Society (www.isoc.org) and the World Wide Web Consortium (www.w3.org). In fact, the technical evolution of the Internet can be traced by looking at the Internet Society's Request For Comments documents (www.rfc-editor.org), the vehicle by which people propose, debate, and agree upon the standards and procedures that make the Internet work.

Here are some Internet buzzwords that you may have seen. They are some of the many standards in use on the Internet and Web today:

- TCP/IP (Transmission Control Protocol / Internet Protocol) – Standard that defines how files are split into packets, routed across the Internet, and put back together again at the other end.
- ASCII (American Standard Code for Information Interchange) – Standard that defines how numbers and letters are represented as bits.
- HTML (Hyper Text Markup Language) – Standard that describes how to mark up text to control its display in a browser.
- HTTP (Hyper Text Transfer Protocol) – Standard that describes how to connect files to one another over the Web via clickable links.
- URL (Uniform Resource Locator) – Standard that

OPEN STANDARDS

provides a method to find a Web page on a server and the server on the Internet; identifies the protocol for accessing it.
- GIF (Graphics Interchange Format), PNG (Portable Network Graphic), and JPEG (Joint Photographic Experts Group) – Standards for image files.
- POP3 (Post Office Protocol 3) – Standard for receiving email.
- SMTP (Simple Mail Transfer Protocol) – Standard for sending email.

Open Standards

Standards define the context and the meaning of a signal in a communication. In a Web page, the bits might represent a word. In an image file, they might be color-squirting directions. In a RealAudio sound file, the bits might represent a phrase of a song. Standards perform the same service for computers that language performs for people – they give us the context (i.e., "Let's speak English") and the meaning of individual words. And just like no one "owns" English, no one should "own" standards, the language of computing.

An *open standard* is a published standard that is possessed by no one and used by all. HTML is an open standard. It is managed by the World Wide Web Consortium, which has responsibility for its dissemination and evolution. But the Consortium does not own it. No one does. Anyone can inspect, criticize, or suggest enhancements to an open standard and any changes must be made by consensus.

A *proprietary standard*, on the other hand, is typically owned by a corporation. Its internals can usually not be inspected. Its use is licensed by its owners. It can be changed at will.

Open vs. Proprietary Standards

The types of streaming audio that we discussed in the Sound and Motion chapter, RealAudio and MP3, illustrate this difference.

You can listen to RealAudio files using a Real client because RealNetworks has specified three things:

- ❐ how the sound is digitized,
- ❐ how the server streams the file to the client, and
- ❐ how the client interprets and plays the file once it arrives.

Such a specification is typically done by writing a standard: a set of rules describing interfaces and processes. This particular standard is a proprietary standard, created and controlled by RealNetworks. RealNetworks invented streaming audio and it owns the RealAudio standard. If you want to play a RealAudio file, you need the RealAudio client; you can't write your own. Likewise, if you want to serve RealAudio files you need RealAudio server software. The specifications that define how the servers talk to the clients are not open to public view and the evolution of the standard is controlled solely by RealNetworks.

MP3 is the other popular flavor of streaming audio on the Web. MP3 is an open standard, developed by a group of companies working through the International Standards Organization (ISO). ISO has published a technical specification of MP3 so anyone can write client software or server software for MP3 files. As a result, many companies have developed client software and many other companies have created Web sites that serve sound files. Since both client software and server software are written to the open MP3 standard, they can successfully communicate with one another even though the software is written by different people.

The MP3 standard typifies a different way of doing business,

OPEN STANDARDS

one based on open rather than proprietary standards. Because the guts of the standard are published for all to see, many different individuals and companies can create different products and services based on the open standard, knowing they will all work together.

If you happen to develop the software that creates MP3 files, you have to pay a royalty fee to the appropriate patent holders, but you can still utilize the standard to write your software. And the people who use your software to create MP3 files, the people who build MP3 sites, and the people who develop MP3 client software to play the files can all utilize the open standard to their heart's content, royalty-free. As a result, an entire new industry has grown up around MP3. Sites with huge numbers of MP3 music files are sprouting all over the Web, giving access to music by all kinds of established and up-and-coming (and completely unheard of) artists. MP3 players have proliferated. So have CD rippers, the software that copies your CD tracks and stores them in much smaller MP3 files on your hard disk for later playback. Ironically, even though RealNetworks invented streaming audio, the big boom in digital music on the Web is MP3; RealNetworks has even come out with its own MP3 player. Such is the power of open standards.

Open Standards and Growth

Over and over again, open standards have proven to be the power that fuels phenomenal growth. Europeans use cellular phones twice as much as Americans. In Finland, wireless phones already outnumber wired ones. The main reason is because Europeans agreed to use a single, open, digital cellular standard. Equipment manufacturers therefore only have to build to one set of specifications and everyone's phones work equally well anywhere in Europe. As a result, business is booming and new services such as messaging and two-way data transfer are rolling out much faster and much more comprehensively in Europe than they are in the United States.

Open standards can grow an entire industry, leaving more room and more opportunity for everyone. And they improve products, because rivals can compete only through price and quality. Most importantly, open standards provide the clarity and stability necessary to create new forms of communication and exchange. They provide an elegant, transparent way for people to interact in a cooperative fashion.

The Power of Cooperation

The Web is a product of the thoughtful cooperation of individuals all over the world. When we think of people cooperating, we often think of a group of people working together as a unit to attain a specific goal. The Web is a marvel of cooperation but ironically it utilizes cooperation so that each one of us can attain our own goals. Agreements to cooperate between people on the Web are constructed so that each person and organization can do its own thing. As Tim Berners-Lee says in *Weaving the Web*, "As long as we accept the rules of sending packets around, we can send packets containing anything to anyone."

On the Web, cooperation results in people doing anything they want, often at cross-purposes. Astrology bits ride the network right along with bits from NASA; Shakespeare rides right next to Beevis and Butthead. When you participate on the Web either as a creator or as a consumer, although you agree to make your computer cooperate in a quite sophisticated and precise manner, what you then do is completely up to you. The more the Web grows in diversity and complexity, the more it comes to resemble the full extravagance, color, and richness of being human.

Cooperation on the Web has enabled an explosion of communication and exchange. We have much to say to one another and much to buy and sell; the wonder is that the cooperation implemented via standards has such a huge payback.

Searching the Web

"... a kind of disorganized Boswell of the human spirit."

– *Vinton G. Cerf*

AS THE MILLENNIUM begins, there are more than seven million sites and more than a billion pages on the Web, enabling the communication of words, pictures, sound, motion, and logic all over the planet. The challenge is finding, in all that overwhelming abundance, the information that is meaningful to you.

If you surf like I do, you first have to make your computer dial into your Internet Service Provider (ISP). As you log on, you hear the dial tone, the number being dialed, the weird Internet song with the octave jump in the middle, some mushy static, and finally the quiet that tells you you're connected. At last, you can check mail, surf, or listen to music. When you're done, you disconnect.

At some point in the future, we'll look back on such a process much like we now look back on the guy in the silent movie who cranks the handle on the front of a Model-T to get it started. At some point, our computers will be continuously connected to the Internet. But now, most are not. In fact, most computers on the planet are not connected to the Internet in any fashion. But if you want to serve files on the Web, you have to put them on a computer that has, among other things, a continuous (i.e., not a dial-up) link to the Internet.

There are a number of ways to do this. Many institutions such as schools, universities and businesses have computers with permanent links to the Internet. If you don't have access to a computer with a permanent link, you can still serve files by using a company that provides such a service. Most ISPs offer a way to serve Web pages, either under their name (e.g., www.my-isp.net/yournamehere/home.html) or under a domain name that you create yourself.

Let's say you want to put up a Web site for a book you just wrote. And let's say your ISP provides a way to host a site with a name of your own choosing. So you register a great domain name like *duomopress.com,* build the proper Web files, and arrange for the files to be served. Congratulations! You have your own Web site!

Then guess what happens? Absolutely nothing.

All action on the Web is initiated by a click on a link which downloads a file, just like all the action on the voice telephone network takes place when one person calls another. Clicking on a link is like dialing a phone number. If no one clicks, it's like a phone that never rings. The files stay right where they are and never see the light of day.

We've talked about the Web providing a medium for the worldwide, instant transmission of text and image and a medium for the broadcast of radio and video, and it does. But in point of fact, true to its pedigree as the telephone company for computers, the files just wait on the server until someone calls for them by clicking on a link. Any number of people at any time from anyplace in the world can click on the link. So the medium can indeed reach a mass, global audience. But nothing happens until someone clicks. The communication is controlled by the actions of the receiver. This method of delivery, called *Pull,* is how information moves on the Web.

Push vs. Pull

If you've ever pitched junk mail without reading it, walked past racks of unsold magazines, or passed up a pile of brochures sitting on a desk, you know something about the information delivery model called *Push*. With Push, the sender creates hundreds or thousands or millions of copies of a message, pushes it out there by phoning, printing, shipping or displaying it, and hopes that at least some people will pay attention. Push is based on chance. Direct mailers, who use a classic push method, are happy when they get a two percent response rate. This method, while ubiquitous, is problematic. The main difficulty is that most of the people the message reaches could care less, so a high percentage of its cost is wasted. As a result, messages that are pushed tend to be crafted to reach the general audience; niche audiences get ignored because their numbers are so small. Finally, with a pushed message, even if you're interested, odds are that when you want the information you can't find it anyway because it came last week and you tossed it, or you left it at work, or you left it at home.

Pull on the other hand, describes an information delivery model based upon demand. You initiate a communication when you want to know something. In Pull, the receiver controls the nature and time of the communication, rather than the sender. The sender waits passively, all dressed up with no place to go, until the receiver initiates the communication by calling, signing up, or sending in a postcard, indicating an interest and a willingness to receive. Communication on the Web is pull-based; nothing happens until the surfer clicks a link and the receiving computer "calls" the sending computer and requests a file. (This is unfortunately not the case with email, as evidenced by the huge amount of junk pushed into our emailboxes.) Communication on the Web is therefore driven by the surfer and is controlled by two things: the interests of the person doing the surfing and that person's ability to find sites of interest.

When you surf, you have to have at least some idea what you're looking for. Information about tin whistles? The common cold? Hip-Hop or Mozart MP3 files? Video from New Zealand? Alternatively, you could go to a site that generates a random link, taking you to a different one of the millions of Web pages out there each time you click. But for the most part, you surf because you are interested in something. The trick, of course, is actually finding sites that are meaningful. And just like you need white pages, yellow pages, and directory assistance services to locate phone numbers, you need catalogs and search engines to locate sites on the Web. You can't pull them until you find them.

Catalogs, Search Engines, and Portals

When you visit a *catalog* such as Yahoo, you will notice three things. You will see a list of clickable, high-level categories such as Arts & Humanities, Computers & Internet, Entertainment, Health, and Science. When you click on any of these, you'll then get a list of clickable subcategories, which when clicked lead to other lists. You can click down as far as you want in selected subcategories until you land on your topic of interest. These clickable catalogs provide to Web users the same service that a Yellow Pages provides to telephone users – a way to find information by category. And like Yellow Pages, catalogs cover specific regions, only the regions are not only cities, they are countries and even continents. Chicago has its own Yahoo, as does Asia, Hong Kong, Mexico, and the UK and Ireland.

When you visit a *search engine* such as Google or Altavista, you will see a space into which you can enter a search request. Search engines can provide search and catalog services because they have built huge databases of information about Web sites. When a Web site is served, the developer typically registers the site with a number of search engines. The search engines then send automated programs called *spiders* to the registered Web address. The spiders send back information on each page that includes the URL, the title of the page, any descriptive information, and all the words that make up the page and how often they occur. That information is then processed to create the searchable databases upon which the catalogs and search features are built.

When you enter a phrase like "tin whistle," the search engine combs through its vast databases looking for Web sites that contain the following:

- ❐ The words "tin" and "whistle" in the title of any Web page.
- ❐ The words "tin" and "whistle" in the description or keyword list. Descriptions and keywords are non-displaying fields added to Web pages by developers specifically so the pages can be found by search engines.
- ❐ The words "tin" and "whistle" in the text.

The search engine then displays a clickable list of the Web pages in its databases that fit the search criteria. From this list you can click on the links and visit the sites.

The final thing you will see when you visit catalogs and search engines are a number of other links to current information and activities (e.g., headlines, weather, stock quotes, sports, travel, classifieds, personals, chat rooms, auctions) and of course links to purchase opportunities (e.g., shopping for DVDs, toys, books, electronics, and computers). Such links are constructed to motivate you to come back to the site day after day to check the headlines, see who won a game, or track your favorite stock. The idea is to make the site attractive enough that you want to come to it every day – that you make it your *portal* to the Internet. On the Web, traffic means delivering eyeballs to advertisers which means money, so such companies strive to provide the best catalog, search, and portal features possible.

Mechanizing Meaning

Nevertheless, finding relevant information on the Web can be a challenge. Search engines must currently resort to insufficient mechanical means such as brute force word searches. As a result, searches often turn up logical but meaningless responses. For example, a search on the term "Chicago Fire" may bring up information on the Chicago Fire soccer team and not information on the historical event. Furthermore, it is often necessary to click on the link and visit the site to see if it will be useful; the site descriptions that show up in search engines are often incomplete or nonexistent.

If you're after a very specific type of information that is easily identifiable by word phrases and that returns a small volume of responses, search engines work just fine. "Mozart Piano Sonatas" is such a query. There's a decent but not overwhelming number of sites with information about Mozart piano sonatas, so it's feasible to look at each one by hand. And search engines can also accept complex search requests. For example, you can tell it to look for all the words, or any of the words, or the words in a specific order. Some search engines also function by querying other search engines and incorporating the all the responses. Or they search known retail sites for a selected object and return responses (including price) from all sites that sell the object.

Ultimately, however, basing searches on word matching alone is simply inadequate. (One search I did a while back returned a lovely *Star Trek* site in Italian. While entertaining to browse, it had nothing to do with my search, even though enough of the words matched – across languages! – to return a response.) There are better ways of finding meaningful sites. The most effective is through the use of *metadata*: information used to aid the identification, description and location of resources on the Web.

Metadata

Metadata is information about information. It is not a new concept; librarians have been using it for years to manage their book collections. Almost every book on the market in the United States today has a virtual gold mine of metadata associated with it in the form of Library of Congress Cataloging-in-Publication information, which includes:

- Author
- Title
- If the book has a bibliography and index
- International Standard Book Number (ISBN)
- If the book is fiction
- Subject category and subcategories
- Copyright
- Library of Congress Control Number
- Cataloging numbers

Because the context of this key information is standardized, it is easy to mechanize. Therefore, you can use computers to search for information about books in a structured and efficient fashion. If you want to find a book by an author named Joe Homer, you can tell the computer to look only in the list of author names. You'll find the book by Joe Homer, not a book about the Greek poet Homer, or a book about Homer Simpson, or a book about famous home runs in baseball history.

The Web is not yet in such an evolved state. In our "Chicago Fire" search, for example, there is no built-in context that allows the Web site developer to identify the nature of the information in the site (e.g., sports vs. history). As Tim Berners-Lee says, "The great need for information about information, to help us categorize, sort, pay for, and own information, is driving the design of languages processed by machines, rather than people. The web of human-readable documents is being merged with a web of machine-understandable data. The potential of the mixture of humans and machines working together and communicating through the Web could be immense." (www.w3.org/People/Berners-Lee-Bio.html/ShortHistory.html)

Sort of Meta

When Web site developers add descriptions and keywords to Web pages they are adding metadata of sorts. Also, when developers register sites with catalogs such as Yahoo, they must pick the category and the precise subcategories for the site before it's added. Here are the categories and subcategories for a technical writing company: "Business and Economy - Companies - Communications and Media Services - Writing and Editing - Technical Writing". Unfortunately, such a categorization resides only in that particular search engine and is not permanently hooked to the site. But within each search engine, you can take advantage of this metadata by searching only within a specific category. For example, searching for "Chicago Fire" within "Arts - Humanities - History" returns links to the great Chicago fire while searching within "Recreation - Sports" returns links about the soccer team. Auction sites and online retailers also offer implicit metadata by the way in which objects are categorized. A search for the word "Mouse" under the "Computer" category will return different links than a search under the "Pets" category! But that is as far as we've gotten.

The real answer to meaningful searching on the Web is this: the creation of a standard method to incorporate metadata in sites, the willingness of developers to describe their sites using standard metadata, and the enhancement of servers, clients, and search engines to take advantage of metadata when fulfilling our search requests.

Real Metadata

Work is, in fact, under way on at least a portion of the solution. A number of groups are developing various standards for the incorporation of metadata into Web sites. One of the more popular metadata schemes is called the Dublin Metadata Core Element Set, better known as the "Dublin Core."

The Dublin Core (purl.org/metadata/dublin_core) is a set of descriptors that can be used to specify the content, intellectual property data, and version information of Web pages. It consists of the following:

Content:
  Title
  Subject and Keywords
  Description
  Resource Type (e.g., home page, novel, poem)
  Source
  Relation (e.g., related resource)
  Coverage (e.g., time period)

Intellectual Property:
  Creator
  Publisher
  Other Contributor
  Rights Management (e.g., copyright)

Version:
  Date
  Format
  Resource Identifier (e.g., URL)
  Language

A developer can add Dublin Core metadata to a Web site using a language called Resource Description Framework (RDF), developed by the World Wide Web Consortium (www.w3.org). It is a language that looks much like the language in which Web pages are developed and is readable by computers.

Metadata such as the Dublin Core not only provides searchable information about a Web site, it contains a clear specification of that information. A Dublin Core date, for example, is defined with the month appearing before the day, so 1999-03-09 means March 9th, not September 3rd. While this may appear trivial, the automated search of metadata by computers requires that the exact meaning of each field be agreed upon. In 1999, when the National Aeronautics and Space Agency crashed a $125 million orbiter space craft into Mars, it was because its engineers were measuring rocket thrusts in feet per second and the on-board computers were executing rocket thrusts in the metric equivalent. That miracle of technology was scuttled by a simple lack of a data definition.

The Dublin Core is good at categorizing text-based materials. But what if you wanted to categorize art? To properly categorize and search for works of art on the Web, you would need to create various categories (and therefore metadata) that included materials and techniques, display guidelines, time period, condition, conservation and exhibition history, any text references, and current location. And what about categorizing and searching satellite images of earth? Metadata for digital images or maps would include categories to describe the geographic location covered by the map as well as information to indicate data quality (e.g., cloud cover for satellite photos).

A number of metadata formats now exist, many of them written in Resource Description Framework. The formats vary from those that are fairly simple to ones that are quite complex. But they have many elements in common, even if they are not called the same thing. The "Creator" descriptor in the Dublin Core might be called "Author" in another metadata scheme or "Artist" in a third; however, they all mean the same thing. Happily, work is also under way to map various metadata schemes to one another. This will enable our computers to do all the searching and translating for us between "Creator" and "Author" and "Artist." This is just the sort of mind-numbing work at which computers excel. When Tim Berners-Lee speaks of a human-machine semantic Web, this is one of the things he means. The humans on the team create metadata to disclose the meaning and the context of Web sites. The computers on the team crank through those metadata words, translating as appropriate. Then, when we do a search, we actually get something resembling what we were looking for.

Metadata schemes are part of the answer to improving meaning on the Web. Another part is provided by the Web site developer who is willing to provide accurate metadata in the first place. Following the idea of "truth in labeling," it's up to the developer to write the metadata accurately enough so that people searching the site can determine whether the site will be of use.

The final part of the answer involves enhancing search engines, servers, and clients to take advantage of the metadata.

The pull-based nature of the Web dictates that we have to locate a site before we can experience it, similar to calling someone on the phone before we can talk to them. Out of the hundreds of millions of files on the Web, metadata has the potential to connect us with the words, pictures, sound, motion, and logic that we really want to see. But right now, it is still mostly a potential. We're stuck with current tools until all the parts of the answer for improving meaning are in place. When that happens, we'll be able to find what we want and the full richness of the Web will truly be ours. Then the only thing we'll have to worry about is the time it takes to download.

Bandwidth and the World Wide Wait

WHEN I MAKE a telephone call from Chicago to our friend Judi in Washington, D.C., the phone company creates a connection between us. The connection starts at my telephone and continues through the wire that goes out the wall to the telephone pole. Then it goes over the wire assigned to my phone number and on to the telephone company central office for my neighborhood. The connection passes across the voice telephone network to a local central office in Washington, D.C., out the wire assigned to Judi's phone number, and on to their house and telephone. She and I can then listen and talk to one another over this connection until we both hang up.

When I send her an email, something similar happens, as the email travels through the telephone company for computers. I dial into my Internet Service Provider (ISP), write the email and click "Send." The file representing my email travels in *packets* (i.e., chunks of a file) from my computer and modem over the telephone wire to my central office. The file then zips to the ISP where it enters the Internet network proper. It is routed to Washington, D.C. to Judi's ISP, where it is stored in her email box. When she dials in to check her email, the message completes its journey to her computer via her central office, telephone wire, and modem.

When I surf, the files of words, pictures, sound, motion, and logic take a similar path. After I click on a link, my browser generates a request for the Web page that goes out via the modem, over the telephone wire to the central office, and on to the ISP, the Internet, and the Web server hosting the Web page. The server serves the files of the Web page and those files travel back to me, going from the server via the Internet to my ISP, to my central office, and over my telephone wire through the modem to my computer, where my browser displays the files.

The Local Loop

The telephone wire to my home is actually a pair of copper wires called a *local loop* that runs from the central office to my home and then back again. When we use our phones to dial into the Internet, this local loop is largely responsible for slowing down response time and turning the World Wide Web into the World Wide Wait.

The classic *dial-up* Internet communication looks like this:

Human
  Computer (i.e., client)
    Modem
      Local Loop (i.e., telephone wire)
        Central Office
          ISP
            Internet network
              Server
                  And then back again:
              Server
            Internet network
          ISP
        Central Office
      Local Loop (i.e., telephone wire)
    Modem
  Computer (i.e., client)
Human

That's how humans use computers to send files over the Internet and that's how the Internet functions as the telephone company for computers.

The telephone network was engineered to carry the human voice, not a bunch of bits. Yet most of us access the Internet with a dial-up connection. That means our use of the Internet involves a trip via a modem across at least part of the voice telephone network – the local loop to the central office. That leg of the trip, the loop between you and the central office, is the most vexing roadblock to the creation of high-speed Internet access. Those millions of miles of local loops, in the ground and on telephone poles, are unfortunately unequal to the task of handling high-speed Internet access. Therefore, a colossal amount of work and investment is required to give us the kinds of wires we need. Communications companies will be spending enormous amounts of money in the next few years to solve this problem.

In order to illuminate and judge the solutions that such companies are proposing for the roadblock of the local loop, let's look at a few simple telephone network characteristics. Understanding these characteristics will make it easier to judge the various high-speed Internet access options that are now becoming widely available.

- All dial-up connections have to pass through at least part of the voice telephone network – the local loop between your home and the central office.
- A local loop can suffer from noise or static, crosstalk, interference, moisture, and critters chewing on the lines. Humans can usually communicate through these disturbances but computers and modems get completely bogged down.
- In a network such as the Internet, the entire download

time is at least as slow as the slowest link in the chain. A file could blaze across the country in milliseconds, but if it has to creep the last mile from the central office to you, the entire download will be just that slow.
- ❏ Much traffic on the Internet is either local or is generated by downloads from a small percentage of very popular Web sites.
- ❏ Surfing is mostly a matter of receiving information. By clicking on a link, you send a very tiny request to the server which then generates a potentially huge download of files. However, future Internet applications such as interactive sound and video may not fit this tiny-upload/huge-download profile.

The local loop presents a gigantic logistical challenge to the delivery of high-speed Internet access. Each local loop is a pair of copper wires (fondly known as the "twisted pair") going to each home via telephone poles or underground cables. In the United States alone there are over 600 million miles of these copper wires. Almost half of all American households use the Internet, most of them dialing up over their local loop. If these local loops are to be upgraded to deliver high-speed access, the wires must be identified, located, and physically manipulated by a technician who must drive to a neighborhood and climb a telephone pole or dig up a buried cable. The local loop is by far the Web's biggest bottleneck; files can move about 170,000 times faster over the Internet's speediest circuits than they can over a local loop.

The local loop is the biggest roadblock to speed but not the only one. On a network where the entire download time for a file is at least as slow as the slowest link, many factors contribute to the World Wide Wait, including slow or busy servers, the distance a file must travel, and congestion on the Internet proper.

The Internet

What does the Internet itself look like? It looks a lot like a telephone network. For most of the last century, the Bell System, in concert with hundreds of smaller, mostly rural telephone companies, wired the United States for voice. Since deregulation, the offspring of the Bell System as well as other players like Sprint and MCI have continued building a series of networks that operate together to deliver local and long distance voice telephone service to the United States and to interconnect with telephone companies in other countries. They also have created a series of private data networks for corporations, universities, and other institutions that work along with and alongside the voice network.

The Internet is a data network built to send packets between servers and clients. With the voice and data networks, it forms our telecommunications infrastructure. Major Internet National Service Providers (NSPs) including AT&T, BBN, PSI, Sprint, and UUNet/MCI, have created a series of high-speed networks called *backbones* that transfer packets representing our files. Backbones are interconnected at Network Access Points (NAPs) to government, regional, and academic networks in the United States as well as similar networks in the rest of the world (e.g., EBONE in Europe). Our ISPs hook into this network as well, which is how we get access. Once you're on the network, you can get to everyone else on the network and they can get to you. To date, the four original NAPs in the United States (Chicago, New York, San Francisco, and Washington, D.C.) have grown to twelve as facilities and traffic have increased.

Not surprisingly, the Web contains a wealth of information about itself. If you're interested in learning more about the structure and future of the Internet and the Web, check out the Internet Society (www.isoc.org) and the World Wide Web Consortium (www.w3.org). Also, you can find a great tour of the Internet at the What Is site (www.whatis.com/tour.htm). And to see terrific graphic visualizations of the various networks of which it is made, see An Atlas of Cyberspaces at www.cybergeography.org or do a search on "visualize internet topology."

The Internet Service Provider (ISP)

On the voice network, we usually deal with one local telephone company and one long distance telephone company to gain access. On the Internet, we gain access through an Internet Service Provider (ISP). However, ISPs provide much more than an Internet connection, including services such as email, Web site hosting, search features, and tech support. People with dial-up connections can easily change their ISPs so competition has improved the services that these companies offer. ISP choice, however, is something that may not survive the delivery of high-speed Internet access; more on that in the chapter on Content and Connection.

Traffic on the Internet

When we talk on the phone, it doesn't take forever for the other person's voice to reach us. When we watch TV, the shows don't broadcast in slow motion. When we listen to the radio, the songs bang out in perfect rhythm. But when we surf the Web, we wait and wait.

If you recall from our earlier discussions, text files are of reasonable size, picture files are much larger, audio files are even larger than that, and video files are the biggest of all. That translates directly to the time it takes for the files to download, making the delivery of the multimedia parts of the Web the most painful. If the Internet were all words, download times would not be an issue. But image, audio, and video files are not only quite large, such files are seeing the most explosive growth.

When the fourth *Star Wars* movie came out in 1999, Apple Computer posted a preview of the movie as a QuickTime file on its site. The file was 25 Megabytes in length and was downloaded more than 23 million times, generating more than 400 trillion bytes of Internet traffic.

Traffic on the Internet is measured in Perabytes (1,000 trillion bytes) per month. As traffic increases, the capacity of the network must increase in order to keep download times reasonable. In effect, in order to cut down travel times, we need to build not only wider highways but wider side streets for our data, which brings us to a discussion of *bandwidth*.

Bandwidth

In his book *The Race for Bandwidth*, Cary Lu defines bandwidth as "a measure of how much information can flow from one place to another in a given amount of time." (Redmond, Washington: Microsoft Press, 1998). Bandwidth, therefore, is as much a matter of capacity as it is of speed. On the Internet, it is purely a matter of capacity since speed is determined by the physics of electricity and light. Capacity, however, is up to us. A high speed line is faster because it allows our bits to march side by side, rather than in single file, so more of them reach their destination in the same amount of time. High-speed lines are fast not because they transmit more quickly but because they are wide enough to transmit more bits at one time. If you're transmitting a voice over a phone line, bandwidth doesn't matter. If you're transmitting information, it matters very much.

If cars were data and highways had bandwidth, we would measure it by the number of cars that could utilize the highway in a certain amount of time. For example, I can drive downtown on the Kennedy Expressway in Chicago at four in the morning in about 10 minutes; if I try the same trip at 5:00 P.M. on a Friday

GETTING THE WEB

evening, it could take an hour and a half. Why? Because the number of cars making the same trip exceeds the bandwidth of the highway. So we all wait. Once bandwidth is exceeded, everything slows down. The solution is to build a highway with adequate bandwidth, maybe one that's 30 or 40 lanes wide. Odds are good that even Chicago traffic wouldn't clog up a highway that wide, but you never know. And we never will, because no one is going to build a 40-lane highway for cars. But we are for data.

On the Internet, we measure bandwidth by measuring how many bits can move from one place to another in one second. We call it bits per second, or *bps*.

Here's a refresher on words just to get you warmed up. These numbers are actually approximations since a Kilo is really 2^{10} or 1024 and so on (that happens when you count only using 0s and 1s):

Thousand = Kilo	1,000
Million = Mega	1,000,000
Billion = Giga	1,000,000,000
Trillion = Tera	1,000,000,000,000
Pera	1,000,000,000,000,000

A connection at a fixed width is just like a highway: the more bits you have, the more time it takes once the bandwidth limit is exceeded. The more media-rich Web sites get, the more traffic they generate and the longer they take to download.

And just like a highway, the alternative to waiting is the creation of connections with bigger bandwidths, allowing more bits to march side by side, like cars on a multilane highway. Sending 28,000 bits through a connection that has a bandwidth of 28,000 bps will take about a second; sending it through a 56,000 bps connection will take only half as long. Browsing a media-rich Web page over a 28K modem connection could take a minute or two; browsing that same page via a direct T1 connection would take only a second or two because it's a much wider road. That's a big difference and communications companies are betting that it's a difference for which people are willing to pay.

Here are the approximate bandwidths of different Internet connections:

28K modem	28,000 bps
56K modem	56,000 bps
T1 line	1,500,000 bps (1.5 Mbps)
T3 line	45,000,000 bps (45 Mbps)
OC3	155,000,000 bps (155 Mbps)
OC12	622,000,000 bps (622 Mbps)
OC48	2,400,000,000 bps (2,400 Mbps or 2.4 Gbps)
OC192+	9,600,000,000+ bps (9,600 Mbps or 9.6 Gbps)

The backbone networks of the Internet are composed of combinations of T1s, T3s, and optical carrier connections (the OCs). Of course, we could all just order T1 lines, but then our phone bills would approach a thousand dollars a month and we'd all have to become mini-ISPs to do the other tasks necessary to manage a direct connection to the Internet. The alternative is to await the high-speed solutions developed by the communications companies.

The work required to deliver universal, high-speed access to the Internet falls into two spheres: speeding up the network proper (backbones, Network Access Points, etc.) and breaking up the bottleneck of the last mile created by our use of the local loop.

Speeding up the Internet Network

The National Service Providers who manage the networks of the Internet are large corporations with access to capital markets so they can invest in new facilities to increase bandwidth. For example, they can install additional high-speed backbones or speed up the routing of traffic through the Network Access Points.

In addition, many companies are implementing a strategy

called *network cashing*, which effectively cuts down traffic by bringing Web content closer to its ultimate destination. This is how it works. As we said earlier, much traffic on the Internet is either local or it is generated by a few very popular Web sites (e.g., AOL, Yahoo). If hundreds of thousands of people sign on in Chicago and they all go to Yahoo.com, the same few Web pages would download over and over again from California. On the other hand, if the network had a copy of Yahoo.com stored on a server in Chicago, it could intercept the request and serve Yahoo from the local copy rather than fetching it from California. The download would go much faster, traffic on the backbone would be reduced, and no one would know the difference. Network caching of the content of very popular sites reduces network congestion and speeds up download time.

Speeding up traffic on the Internet proper is a technically sophisticated and difficult undertaking. But it pales in comparison to the work required to break the bottleneck of the local loop.

Speeding Up the Local Loop

If you stand outside your house or apartment, you will probably see three types of wires entering the building: telephone, cable TV, and electrical. Telephone lines are already widely used to access the Internet and cable TV isn't far behind.

The Internet was able to grow as fast as it did because so much of the infrastructure was already in place. When I started surfing in 1995, I didn't need to buy a computer; I already had one. And I didn't have to order a phone line. All I needed was a modem, an ISP account, and some software. The Internet access that most of us have today is very similar. The modems and machines have gotten faster but everything else remains the same.

As we have said, the act of dialing into an ISP puts us on the voice network. Although that leg is only a small part of the path, it slows down the entire transmission. So even if well-heeled National Service Providers create the speediest backbones in the world, dial-up access will be limited by the tiny bandwidth available on the voice network. The 56K modems that are popular today make the absolute best use they can of that sliver of bandwidth, but access won't get faster until we break the voice bandwidth barrier. Or until we do something completely different, like converting our bits into color rather than sound and sending them through our cable TV cables, or converting them to radio waves and sending them through the air.

As the millennium begins, the Internet is still a network of institutions such as governments, schools, universities, corporations, and ISPs, with direct, high-speed connections to the Internet. In fact, ISPs exist mainly to get the rest of us onto this institutional network. But since our access piggybacks on the voice network, we're limited by the 56K ceiling. It took decades and a massive monopoly to get the country wired for voice; wiring for data isn't going to happen overnight.

In the Interim

In the meantime, the industry is moving ahead with interim solutions that make things better but not ideal. These solutions can all be described as *broadband* – broad bandwidth connections that accommodate high-speed data transmission. They are meant to provide to homes and small enterprises the high-speed Internet access that large institutions already enjoy. Broadband access provides not only high speeds, it provides access that is "always on." No more dialing into your ISP, sitting through the busies, and waiting for the connect. If you want to surf, you just launch the browser and off you go. As Tim Berners-Lee says, it makes using the Internet less like using a lawn mower and more like using a pen.

Because implementing broadband access is such a huge logistical undertaking, the costs will vary for each of these solutions,

So will the way in which corporations make and recover their investments. When I dial into the Internet using my 56K modem, the telephone company doesn't have to do anything. But if I want to break the voice bandwidth barrier on my local loop, not only do I need a new modem, the telephone company needs a new modem in the central office that can hear more than voice frequencies. It also has to make sure that the copper wires in the local loop are of high quality. If not, a technician will have to climb a pole or dig up a cable. And that will have to happen not just for me but for the millions of other people who eventually will want broadband access.

Speed in Both Directions

The quest for high-speed, broadband access is currently driven by the World Wide Web and its rich multimedia components of images, sound and motion. The broadband solutions seen today reflect that drive. The two front runners, Asymmetric Digital Subscriber Line (ADSL) and cable TV access, both facilitate speedy downloading but not equally speedy uploading. That's not a problem for surfing because it's all on demand and a matter of a tiny request generating a huge download. Email and instant messaging applications upload files to the ISP but they are text-based and small. However, once we get the bandwidth to receive decent sound and video, someone will invent an instant messaging application (imagine it – Barbie WebCam!) whereby kids can not only send each other text but also live sound and video. Then they will be able to see each other making faces and hear each other talk, and once again the local loop could be a bottleneck, only this time a bottleneck of uploading rather than downloading.

The point is, the interim broadband solutions we see today are just that: ways to squeak additional bandwidth out of the existing infrastructure of local loops and cable TV. The Internet is still in its infancy and still very much shaped by the telephone network. Dial-up access allows the Internet to crawl; interim broadband solutions allow it to toddle along on its training wheels. But the ultimate in access is not even close to implementation. All we can hope for (and demand as consumers and stockholders) is that these interim solutions improve the situation today without compromising a better solution for tomorrow, and without compromising the integrity of the network itself (more on that topic in the Content and Connection chapter).

ADSL and cable TV access are the two most popular interim broadband solutions; some combination of either with fiber optics is probably the optimum wired configuration. But there are other alternatives which don't involve wires at all: wireless and satellite. Let's now look at all of these broadband solutions in more detail.

BROADBAND SOLUTIONS

Asymmetric Digital Subscriber Line (ADSL) and the Poor, Deaf Phone Company

When you dial into your ISP, the telephone company can handle your call and get it to the right place because your modem creates sounds within the frequency range of the human voice. If you hit the A above Middle C on a piano, the piano strings would vibrate 440 times in one second (440 cps). The telephone network can transmit and reproduce sounds between 300 and 3,300 cps, a bit above Middle C to a little higher than three octaves above Middle C. When your modem squawks, it squawks within that range and the phone company can transmit those squawks to your ISP. But if the modem generates any sounds above or below that range, they would be lost in the transmission.

However, this voice frequency range takes up less than half of one percent of the frequency range that the copper wires of your local loop can transmit. Even though the voice network wouldn't know what to do with it, the copper wire itself can transmit frequencies up to around one million cps (1 Mhertz). So if you tried to use that other 99 percent without special equipment, the signal (e.g., file) would be lost; it is beyond the range of what the voice telephone network can transmit. Humans can't hear much above 30,000 cps; the voice telephone network can't hear much above 3,300 cps. Using the other 99 percent means using frequencies so high-pitched that they can't be heard and transmitted by the voice network.

ADSL is the most popular entry in a family of DSL technologies that take advantage of the other 99 percent of the frequency range of the local loop. ADSL is implemented via a pair of modems that can hear the full bandwidth of the wire, one at the telephone company central office and the other at your end. The ADSL modem is smart enough to send both voice and data. It sends the voice signal through the traditional 1 percent frequency range of the local loop and sends data through the other 99 percent. Downloads travel at very high speeds, up to around 6 Mbps; uploads however, travel slower, around 640 Kbps.

The ADSL connection is asymmetric – it is structured to allow a much greater bandwidth for downloading than for uploading. That works great for surfing, since very little goes up but a whole lot comes down. However, when we start sending sound and video interactively to each other, the upload constraint could become an issue. The other problem with ADSL is the limited length of the local loop. It doesn't work if you are more than two or three miles away from the central office. It also doesn't work if your local loop is noisy or has been chewed by critters. However, one version of ADSL (G.lite) is designed to run on noisier lines, albeit at slower speeds (1.5 Mbps). But if you are close to a central office, ADSL provides a great way to get high-speed, always-on access.

Cable TV

The other leading broadband solution uses your cable TV line rather than your phone line. It takes the colorful approach of converting your bits into colors rather than sound and sending them as one of the channels in the cable feed to your home.

With cable TV, you access the Internet via a cable ISP that has its own direct connection to the Internet. The cable ISP takes bits and converts them into colors (i.e., analog video signals) and sends them to you on a cable channel. The cable coming in through your wall goes to a splitter rather than to the cable box. There the data channel is split from the regular cable feed; the cable feed goes on to the cable box and TV and the data goes on to the cable modem. The cable modem turns the colors in the video signal back into bits and sends the bits on to your computer.

Like ADSL, cable access is faster on the download than it is on the upload. Likewise, it provides an Internet connection that is always on. One of the problems with cable access is that the download time you actually experience is a function not only of the bandwidth of the connection but of how much everyone else in the neighborhood is downloading. Internet cable access is delivered by bringing into each neighborhood a fiber-enhanced cable feed, to which the cable from your home is connected. All the people connected to that one feed share its 10 Mbps bandwidth. If you share the feed with 50 other people who love to read books in the evening, your downloads will probably be speedy. If you share it with 500 or 1,000 or 2,000 other people who love to download video, you may be better off with your old dial-up connection. Additionally many cable companies don't offer dial-up service to your account usable while traveling. Furthermore, they don't yet offer a choice of ISPs or modems. You use what they give you. This is an issue of some concern and we discuss it in the chapter on Content and Connection. But cable TV access is a way to high-speed, always-on access that is gaining in popularity.

Fiber Optics

The last wired broadband option is fiber optics. Fiber can carry millions of megabits a second; high speed Internet backbones are all fiber optic carriers. Rather than using a modem to wiggle electricity in a copper wire or colors in a cable, fiber optic lines use lasers to wiggle light, turning the light on and off billions of times a second in a pattern that maps to the bits in the file being transmitted. The problem, of course, is that most of us have copper local loops. To replace more than 600 million miles of copper with fiber is a job communications companies may not be willing to take on. Furthermore, light-wiggling devices are needed as well – the optical equivalent of a modem. Fiber is great for new buildings and developments which have to be wired from scratch. If it happens for the rest of us, it will probably happen as fiber to the neighborhood with a connection to existing facilities to the home.

So far, we've seen our bits encoded as sound, color, and light. Why not radio waves?

Wireless Options

That's exactly what Local Multipoint Distribution Services (LMDS) does. It is a wireless system designed to deliver data through the air at millions of bits per second. A receiver is placed on your rooftop in a fixed location that has a good line of sight to a base station antenna; the antenna sends bits encoded as radio waves to your receiver and then to your computer. LMDS is unfortunately limited by noise caused by walls, hills, and water.

Another wireless option uses transmissions from satellites to send radio waves to small receivers on housetops. Satellite systems have huge bandwidth capabilities but they also involve massive deployment costs and are still considered experimental.

Finally, the cell phone has possibilities for evolving into a broadband medium. It faces the same hurdle as the voice telephone network, since it was engineered to carry the human voice, not data. Nevertheless, considering the huge infrastructure investment needed in wired broadband, it remains an interesting alternative.

Accessibility Issues

We think of the telephone as being ubiquitous – everyone has one. But that's not the case, especially in rural areas. Also, the local loop may be too noisy, making it unusable for data transmission. These days, in rural areas, the cost of telephone service resembles the price of providing it. If it costs tens of thousands of dollars to lay wire to your house, you may just have to pay that much if you want a phone. If you're already wired, it's not a big deal. If you're not, it is a big deal.

In the old days, when the Bell System and the independent telephone companies originally wired the country, they used a cost structure that enabled urban areas to subsidize rural areas and business services to subsidize residence services. As a result, the phone companies made money yet everyone was able to afford a telephone, even if the phone company had to run a wire hundreds of miles just for one house. That's not the way things are today. Cost structures in a competitive environment are usually based on the cost of providing the service, so companies tend to invest in services with big paybacks, leaving some customers with either no service or with a service they can't afford. The cost structures used by the communications companies delivering broadband services will determine in large part how widely such services are offered. How granular is the service from which a company must make a profit? What subsidizes what? These questions are all opportunities for civic debate and the answers that materialize will help determine the extent and quality of our broadband access to the Internet.

Cost and Convergence

Cost structures, and more generally, the business models used by communications companies, will determine the nature and quality of the services they provide as well as their accessibility. Let's say a phone company offers always-on, high-speed Internet access, data services, and voice telephone service (most of which is digitized anyway once it leaves the central office). And let's say that both myself and my friend Judi in Washington, D.C. have some software, a microphone, and a speaker that allows us to send interactive sound files through the Internet. We can then use this setup to talk back and forth. If we do this, will we still need telephones? And what about the phone company? I'm using one of their services to supplant another. How should they bill me? In what services should they be investing their capital?

A similar convergence is occurring in cable TV, with cable Internet access giving us the ability to download video on the Internet through the data cable feed as well as video through the traditional cable feed. Does that mean that the cable ISP becomes an entertainment company? Some cable TV companies also offer telephone service. Does that mean they are turning into telephone companies? And what effect will the emergence of digital high-definition TV have? Being able to turn print, images, audio, video, telephone service, TV and movies into bits has great potential for making us and our communications and entertainment industries fairly crazed for some time to come.

Why Bandwidth Matters

Cars have been around for almost a century and we still have huge daily traffic jams. On the other hand, it's a lot easier to lay a fiber optic cable than it is to build a highway. But why is bandwidth important? Why can't we all just be more patient with the Web and sit through the wait? For a few reasons.

Thomas Friedman, in his book *The Lexus and the Olive Tree*, says that the first of the "Eight Habits of Highly Effective Countries" is being wired. "Bandwidth in the late 1990s is important for commerce in the same way that railroads were important in the 1890s and seaports were in the 1790s. It's the way you sell your product." (New York: Farrar Straus Giroux, 1999).

Bandwidth also enables new ways to communicate. Current bandwidth on the Internet handles words quite well but the same cannot be said for images, sound and motion. For us to fully enjoy the riches of the Web, we'll need faster connections. Streaming video is a perfect example. It exists, but its poor resolution and small footprint inhibit it from many important uses. It may be fine for a talking-head news program but would not be adequate as a way to put a lecture online. While we could see the head of the teacher, we might not be able to make out printed words, visual aids or other demonstrations. An entire class of products, the "university on demand," is just one that awaits the arrival of broadband.

We also need faster connections so that new methods of communication and exchange can flower. Fast and always-on connections enable a different level of interaction. For example, voice telephone service on the Internet only works if you have a connection that is always on. And products that deliver interactive video will not take off until a critical number of us have high-speed, always-on access with upload speeds as fast as download speeds. When that happens, we'll all be able to talk to one another like they do on *Star Trek*, looking at a monitor and seeing the person to whom we're talking.

When paper and movable type were invented, book shops sprang up everywhere, creating a marketplace in which ideas could travel by being swapped, bought and sold. Commerce led; culture followed. With broadband access, we bring image, sound and motion into a similar arena and put at least some of the power of broadcast into the hands of the individual. And since this revolution is taking place in the information age, we as consumers, shareholders, and citizens have at least some chance to affect how broadband content and connection are delivered.

Content and Connection

BROADBAND ACCESS to the Internet is finally becoming available in our neighborhood. When we sign up for it, we will have Internet access that is high-speed and always on. That will be great. But what will happen when the younger members of the household go online using their favorite software? We subscribe to America On Line (AOL), an Internet Service Provider that supplies rich content as well as a dial-up connection to the Internet. The children love the content, especially the enhanced instant messaging, chat rooms, user profiles, and easy home page creation. But when they launch AOL after we get broadband access, will they be able to get AOL content via our new high-speed connection or will the software still look for a modem and attempt to dial into AOL the old way? This question highlights the problem of combining both *content* and *connection* into a single product – a practice known as *bundling* – as we move into a world of broadband access to the Internet.

Bundling

AOL started out as an online service well before the World Wide Web splashed onto the scene and so it has a tradition of combining content and connection. It didn't take long, however, for AOL to realize that people who already had a connection to the Internet through work, school, or another Internet Service Provider (ISP), might still want to access AOL content. So it began the Bring Your Own Access program, a means to provide AOL content – for about half the price but with all the advertising – to those folks who already had their own connection. With Bring Your Own Access, AOL *unbundled* content from connection. Because AOL unbundled content, we can set up our current AOL software to connect via TCP/IP rather than through the dial-up AOL network, thereby retaining access to AOL content when we move to our new broadband connection.

AOL has unbundled content; it has not, however, unbundled connection. You can get content alone for half the price. But if you want an AOL connection, content comes with it, whether you want it or not. This may be an annoying situation, but with dial-up access to the Internet, it's not a big deal. If you don't like the service or the bundling you get from an ISP like AOL, you can sign up with another, choosing from just about any ISP reachable with a local phone call. However, the advent of broadband access could change this freedom of choice, because of the bundling of content and connection with the broadband facilities themselves.

Bundling in a Broadband World

Today, high-speed, broadband access to the Internet typically comes in two flavors: via a cable from a cable television company or via a Digital Subscriber Line (DSL) from a telephone company. And once a cable or telephone company goes to the trouble (e.g., installing or upgrading wire and installing special modems) to get you connected, that company would really like to see your cable or phone line hooked directly to an ISP in which it has an interest. A number of large telephone and cable companies are forging agreements with large ISPs (e.g., AT&T and excite@home for cable; SBC and Prodigy for DSL) to provide Internet access services for their customers. There's no problem with that. You need an ISP between you and the Internet; the ISP performs a number of critical services without which your connection would not work. The ISP may also provide gigabytes of content you could probably happily do without or easily find elsewhere, including email, Web hosting, chat, instant messaging, sports information, news groups, e-commerce, headlines, weather, stock quotes, search engines, advertising, and entertainment news and reviews. The question now is, if you buy broadband access from such a cable or telephone company, will you still be able to choose your own ISP?

Bundling Access and ISPs

When cable and telephone companies sign agreements with ISPs to provide Internet services, the obvious temptation is twofold: first, to sell the ISP's services to every home to which they install broadband access; second, to bundle all sorts of features and content with the broadband connection – and charge you one price. Why? Because that's where the money is. By bundling ISPs with access and by bundling content with connection, telephone and cable companies automatically sell ISP services and content that they would otherwise have to sell on the open market. And if they require the use of proprietary rather than standard software, they also gain an army of captive eyeballs to which they can deliver advertising.

Such a setup forces consumers to buy a product they may or may not want (a specific ISP and its content) in order to get something they do want (broadband access). It could expose consumers to unwanted advertising. It fails the "truth in advertising" convention since there is no technical reason to require bundling of ISPs or content with access. Yet that is how it's often pitched. And most critically, it removes the driving force of competition as a motive to improve the quality of the product. A bundled product can be lousy but not suffer a loss of market share because people have no choice in the matter.

If you've ever been on a tour and had the tour bus take you to a restaurant that just happened to be owned by the tour bus company, you've been bundled. Maybe the restaurant was fine; maybe it wasn't. It certainly had no reason to improve its food. The point is, you had no choice. The bus could have dropped you off and let you pick your own restaurant. The driver could have made recommendations or even stopped in front of a favored restaurant. But the choice of restaurant would still have been yours. Instead, the bus company used its momentary control over your whereabouts to sell a product it might not otherwise have been able to sell.

There are more than 6,500 independent ISPs in the United States today, and thousands more worldwide, all competing against one another and thinking up new products and services. Some differentiate themselves by delivering a bare-bones, speedy, reliable connection to the Internet at a reasonable price. Others differentiate themselves by their varied content. For example, some ISPs offer customized services to communities of people who have a common interest (language, culture, sports teams, etc.). Known as "affinity ISPs," they offer an Internet connection as well as content tailored to the interest of the community. Some people are happy to sign up with content-rich ISPs (e.g., affinity ISPs, AOL) while others prefer the simple joy of a fast, reliable connection to the Internet. In a dial-up world, if you don't happen to like an ISP's services or its bundled content, you just sign up with another ISP. In a broadband world, this freedom of choice is not yet guaranteed. Choice of ISP should not be dictated by the company that has the monopoly franchise (cable or telephone) to lay the wire to the home.

The roll-out of broadband presents a perplexing situation because it does involve a heavy investment in facilities (e.g., upgraded wires) as well as sophisticated coordination between telephone companies, cable companies, and ISPs. However, the situation should not be an excuse for cable and telephone companies to structure their offerings in a way that forces purchase of an ISP and content that rightly should be marketed separately.

Public Networks Connect

A "public" network is a network that provides services to the general public. Its services are universally available and the value of the network lies in its ability to connect each user to all other users. Public networks have historically been content-neutral; they are about universal and complete connection, not about content. The Internet is a public network and the ISP is the means by which we all gain access to this public network.

Let's think about two familiar public networks: the voice telephone network and the road network. Telephones and roads are facilities open to the public that offer pure, complete network connections. They are content-neutral, as long as your behavior is within the law. When you make a telephone call, your telephone company provides you with a connection; the content of the call – your conversation – is totally up to you. You can call anyone anywhere on the planet and you can say anything you want. Anyone can call you and say anything they want. The telephone company does not monitor the conversation; it does not make the connection clearer if it happens to like what you are saying. The same is true when you drive across country. You can get from anywhere to anywhere just by going from road to road. Nobody restricts access. Nobody closes roads because they might not like where they lead. The object of a public network is to offer a connection that is efficient, complete, and content-neutral and the Internet is a public network.

Content, Connection and Convergence

The bundling of ISPs and content with broadband access is made more crucial by the phenomenon of convergence: the blurring of traditional boundaries between print, images, audio, video, telephone service, TV, and movies. The more that each of these is represented as bits in files, the more inclination there will be to make the delivery mechanism the same. Wiggle the bits one way, you get a Web page. Wiggle them another way, they become a radio broadcast. Wiggle them a third way, they become a TV show. And they all can in some manner be delivered via the Internet, especially an Internet to which most people have high-speed broadband access.

The stakes are high; this business has a huge potential and corporations are busy dividing up the turf of these new markets. That's great as long as the "public" nature of the Internet is not compromised. In a traditional broadcast network, content and connection are happily joined because that is the nature of the business. It is a private, not a public network; there is no requirement for open access or universal connectivity. A television network owns the content (i.e., the TV shows) and sends the broadcast of its content out through its private broadcast network to its network affiliates, who deliver the broadcast to us. But what happens when a number of centralized, private networks such as TV broadcast and cable networks crunch into the distributed, decentralized public network that is the Internet?

History Repeats Itself

In the United States in the early 1900s, when telephone service was first proliferating, a number of different telephone companies competed against one another, much like today. Only their networks were not interconnected; initially, you could only talk on the telephone to the people who subscribed to the same telephone company as you did. It was the voice telephone network's version of bundling content (i.e., conversation) with connection. The telephone network at that time was in fact not a public network but a series of fragmented, private ones. This looniness eventually resolved itself into the completely interconnected national and international public voice telephone network we know today. This network has served us well for more than one hundred years and continues to serve, represented for most of us by the thin strand of copper wire that comes in from the telephone pole.

The Internet requires a much fatter connection in order for us to send and receive all the bits we have to exchange with one another. Great as it is, the Internet is still very much in its infancy. At some point in the future, most of us will have broadband access at speeds probably ten times faster than what's available today. We'll be able to have our packets switched to a different ISP with a phone call, just like we do today with our long distance carriers. All content (free or otherwise) will be available via any connection. We will consider quaint such practices as having to go through a certain connection in order to access specific content. And we will pay for at least some of that content.

The Pricing Issue

When you get right down to it, the bundling of content and connection is really a pricing issue. With their Bring Your Own Access program, AOL is effectively charging for content, albeit content that is laden with advertising, which makes the subscriber's experience somewhat ironic. In an ideal world, we would pay one price for content, another for connection, or a third, if we choose, for both. Such a pricing strategy on the part of all content-driven ISPs would not only go a long way toward helping keep the Internet a truly public network, it would sharpen the content through competition and make it truly accessible to anyone on the Internet, not just those with the right connection.

Such a pricing strategy would undoubtedly also improve the connection as well; if AOL's dial-up connection service had to stand alone as a product separate from AOL content, I doubt very much that the busy signals we've experienced would be so plentiful. AOL is now offering enhanced multimedia content (AOL Plus). It is also offering broadband connection via DSL (AOL Plus DSL); broadband cable connections and broadband wireless connections are in the works. AOL's broadband bundling appears to be much like its dial-up bundling – content is unbundled but connection is not. Enhanced multimedia (i.e., "broadband") content is unbundled and accessible (for a price) through any broadband access. But broadband connection is still tied to content; if you get DSL from AOL, you get AOL content whether you want it or not. That means that DSL and other broadband offerings from AOL will not be made to stand on their own and will not be open to market competition to control quality and price. But that doesn't have to be the case.

The Infrastructure Challenge

The Internet is the telephone company for computers, a key part of our information infrastructure and a national and global resource. Providing widespread broadband access to it will be a tremendous logistical undertaking, involving the laying or upgrading of millions of miles of wiring, and the installation, where appropriate, of wireless technologies. The current broadband offerings (e.g., DSL, cable) are just round one. Like computer processor speed, the more we have, the more we'll use and the more we'll want. The challenge to cable and telephone companies is to get that infrastructure built and get it built fast. As consumers, citizens, and stockholders, we can encourage investment in the necessary facilities to create high-speed connections to the Internet and shape the business and pricing models used for this investment. And we can use what influence we have to speed the demise of the bundling of facilities, content, and connection.

The more we understand the issues and pitfalls of bundling in a broadband world, the better able we will be to ensure the continued health of the public network that is the Internet.

Part III

Part III explores the ways in which the Internet shapes communication, exchange, and ultimately, us.

GETTING THE WEB

Individuals in Conversation

IN THE EARLY months of the new millennium, Cisco Systems, Inc., the maker of much of the equipment that runs the Internet, ran a series of TV commercials. In each, we saw a succession of people from all over the planet, of varying races, genders, and ages, often in native garb and habitat, looking at the camera and asking, "Are you ready?"

These commercials capture two crucial elements of the Internet. The first, obviously, is its global reach. The second, not so obviously, is the importance of – and the challenge to – the individual. The lad by the garden, the girl in the forest, the elderly Asian man, the woman in the marketplace, as well as you and I, all will determine how the Internet evolves and consequently how it effects us.

Communication and Exchange

The Internet empowers the individual like no other technology before it because the Internet bestows on us a planet-wide audience for communication and exchange. This is what Christopher Locke says about communication and exchange in *The Cluetrain Manifesto* (www.cluetrain.com):

> A few thousand years ago there was a marketplace. Never mind where. Traders returned from far seas with

spices, silks, and precious, magical stones. Caravans arrived across burning deserts bringing dates and figs, snakes, parrots, monkeys, strange music, stranger tales. The marketplace was the heart of the city, the kernel, the hub, the omphalos. Like past and future, it stood at the crossroads. People woke early and went there for coffee and vegetables, eggs and wine, for pots and carpets, rings and necklaces, for toys and sweets, for love, for rope, for soap, for wagons and carts, for bleating goats and evil-tempered camels. They went there to look and listen and to marvel, to buy and be amused. But mostly they went to meet each other. And to talk. . . . Markets are conversations. Trade routes pave the storylines. Across the millennia in between, the human voice is the music we have always listened for, and still best understand.

If your interests, your business, or your mission in life lay within the realm of communication or exchange, the Internet is the tool for you. The human voice may only show up as a squiggle of words on a computer monitor, but it is the human voice nonetheless and represents at least some portion of a human presence. We pass files back and forth between our computers in order to engage in a conversation. It is the conversation that counts, not the technology; the technology just lets it happen. Creating a telephone company for our computers has a significant impact on the way we live precisely because we spend so much of our time communicating and exchanging. On the Internet, the vast complexity and storage capacity of computers fuses with the reach of the telephone network, dramatically enriching our conversations. This gives each of us the power not just to contact anyone on the planet – we can do that now, one person at a time, simply by making a telephone call. The Internet gives us a much grander platform for conversation. It gives us a platform for conversation that can hold a huge and complex repository of words, pictures, sound, motion, and logic, that anyone can explore and respond to, at any time they want, in any way they want. And the effects of these enriched conversations and the possibilities that they open up will endure long after the conversations end.

The Power of Publishing

One way to start a conversation is to publish. The power to publish is essentially the power to communicate – a power that writing bestows – with a mass audience. In the past, the power to publish was held only by governments and corporations. Now, any individual or organization can create a work and gain direct access to a vast audience with whom it can communicate.

To each individual and organization on the planet, the Web gives the power to:

- Publish and read complex repositories of thought and to enter into a dialog on that thought.
- Publish and view visual representations of knowledge, image and art.
- Broadcast or receive music, radio and video from anywhere at any time.

On the Web, people are continuously offering hundreds of thousands of works to the public that might not otherwise have seen the light of day. Many of these works are peculiar, to say the least, but many others are quite wonderful and add to our deposit of cultural, intellectual and spiritual wealth. As Robert Reid says in *Architects of the Web*, the Internet was always about "the exchange of ideas – of all ideas without constraints imposed by popularity or production value thresholds. And since the shelf was infinite, there was no harm in piling it high with the outpourings of anybody who felt like they had something to outpour.

If only two or three people found enough value in a particular site to pluck its pages from the shelf, they at least would be enriched for it, its author would get an audience, and some idea or creation that would not otherwise have had one would gain a voice." (New York: John Wiley and Sons, 1997).

The Power To Exchange

The Internet also gives each individual the power to transact business – another power that writing bestows – with a global marketplace. One of the uses of conversation is making a buck and there are plenty to be made having conversations on the Internet. In the past, exchanges were limited by geography, lack of information, and the cost of promotion to distant customers. Now, with fees for online retailing plummeting, any individual or organization can create a product or a service and gain direct access to at least some portion of the worldwide marketplace. The maker of woolen blankets in the west of Ireland, the blacksmiths of Nepal, the small press in Chicago, all have the power to create and utilize direct Web relationships with a world market. This obviously benefits sellers but also benefits buyers as they can easily find as well as transact directly with the source of the objects they desire. And the Web gives the power not only to participate in markets, but to create them – a lucrative business as the founders of such auction sites as eBay have found out.

The Creator's Tool of Choice

The Internet is still in its infancy. The more each individual is able to grasp its possibilities for communication and exchange and participate not only as a surfer but as a creator, the more we can all realize the full potential of the Web as well as our own. And fortunately, it's not that hard. It all comes down to using files of words, pictures, sound, motion, and logic to create a conversation. We all have the chance to make our voices heard in a fresh and uncensored manner and to hear the voices of those who choose to respond.

If all you want to do is surf the Web, you can use your computer, your cell phone, a palm-held device, or any other appliance that may come on the scene. But if you want to be on the Web as a creator, the computer will always be the tool of choice. The computer offers a tool of almost unlimited storage and complexity so that we may digitize words, pictures, sound, motion, and logic to our hearts content and offer our creations to the world via the Web.

Using Files for Communication and Exchange

If you could see every possible activity on the Web in terms of people creating conversations by moving files back and forth between their computers, it might be easier to figure out how to get some files out there yourself. Sometimes the communication and exchange is purely digital and the entire experience can be completed on the Web (e.g., surfing, emailing, downloading music or software). Other times the Web mediates a communication or exchange on a product or service that exists outside the digital world (e.g., buying concert tickets, blue jeans or a book online; participating in an online auction; checking the exhibits and times of a museum). Either way, you use the Internet to conduct a conversation with another individual so you can communicate, buy, or sell.

Files of words and pictures form the heart of what we know as the Web. Almost any document that exists on a computer can be turned into an HTML file (or a PDF file to maintain specific formatting) and served to the world. Today we also have Web radio broadcasts, MP3 downloads, streaming video and Internet telephony. How can you use files of words, pictures, sound and motion to start your conversations?

You can use files of logic (smart servers and clients) for online retailing, business-to-business e-commerce, and even the creation of markets. Various auction sites like eBay are examples of people using software and the Web to create markets. If you go to eBay as a buyer or a seller, you know that other people will also be there, with goods to buy and sell. EBay makes its money, like marketplaces of old, by providing a place for people to meet and by taking a little off the top of each sale transacted. New markets are springing up daily, especially in the business-to-business arena, with suppliers setting up sites for the industries they serve. Unlike the marketplaces of old, markets on the Internet are independent of geography and even independent of time since they can function around the clock.

Technically, it's all quite complex and sophisticated. Conceptually it's a simple matter of moving files back and forth between servers and clients to engage people in communication and exchange.

The joy of the Web is that storage is almost infinite and information only has to be served once for everyone to get it. And there is little if any marginal cost since ten thousand visits to a Web site cost about the same as one. The Web offers unique opportunities to those who are clever enough to figure out how to leverage its particular ability to connect hard disks all over the planet. The young college student who invented Napster.com did exactly that. Napster is a site that allows people to trade MP3 files directly with one another. You have an MP3 file on your hard disk; I have one on mine. Via Napster, we can find out about each other's files and effect a possibly illegal trade. The point is, the guy who invented Napster figured out a way to exploit the fact that all the hard disks on the Internet are connected. As a result, music is flying between people all over the Web, he's the object of a high-profile copyright suit, and intellectual property law will never be the same.

On the Web, information is freed from paper and trade routes become digital. If you think that this will generate a deeply structural change in the way we communicate and do business, you're right. And if you think that you are going to have to crank up your imagination to really make use of the opportunities the Web has to offer, you're right again. But all such talk is just a grand pile of flapdoodle until that special moment when you get the tickle of the epiphany that it really could mean something to you and what you care about and what you do.

Visualizing Discourse

The Web is a key venue for conversations enabling communication and exchange, but not the only one. The non-Web components of the Internet, including email, instant messaging, discussion lists and news groups, are other crucial vehicles for discourse. The Internet makes it easy to debate. Even a mechanism as simple as email can be a powerful force for dialog. And instant messaging software has created a quick and easy way to literally have conversations online. If you download the software and fill up your "buddy" list with the logons of the people with whom you want to talk, you can send and receive messages almost instantly. While much of the instant messaging I've seen is dedicated to gossip and the arrangement of social events, it could be used for almost anything. For example, one of our local teachers tells her students that she will be online at a certain time on certain evenings; if they need help they can ask her questions and she will tutor them online.

Like email and instant messaging, discussion lists and newsgroups enable conversation, allowing people with common interests to question, answer, examine, diagnose, debate, resolve, praise, excoriate, and rant to their heart's content. And this opportunity to carry on is typically open to anybody. You can post your opinion almost anywhere you'd like. Your interest is what drives your contribution and your content is your credential. As a result of this huge amount of free-flowing information, people can reach consensus much faster, and usually with a better result, than they otherwise would have.

Internet Time

"Internet time is measured in months, not years!" the hype often goes. There is actually something to it, however, for the very reason that the increased flow of information allows people to get to conclusions and consequent action much faster. The Internet's zero marginal cost and near-instantaneous speed allow people to work through complex issues in a short time, making the trip from information to conclusion significantly quicker. Here's one small example. One night when I was online, I got an email from a visitor to our Web site *Building a School Web Site* (www.wigglebits.com). It was from Klaus in Australia; he had a question about where to download a graphics program. I gave him a location, and as he was still online, he took a look but couldn't find what he wanted so he wrote back. I mentioned another location. He responded and I made one more suggestion. A few emails, a little bit of time, one individual to another, even though we were complete strangers, and a small problem was resolved. Klaus found his software so he could move forward with his project and I got a big kick out of talking to someone on the other side of the planet.

On the Internet, we have instant access to all the information on the Web as well as access to all the people who give us their emails for purposes of communication. This repository of power and complexity that we have invited into our homes and onto our desktops, laps, and palms can generate quite a blitz of information and conversation. And the people who take advantage of it to move forward with their mission are the ones with their foot on the gas pedal, creating the phenomenon of Internet time. Of course, Internet time is really nothing more than how long something really should have taken anyway. When I published this book, one of the things I needed was a Library of Congress Control Number. I wrote for the forms and waited three weeks for them to arrive. Had I filled them out and sent them back to the Library of Congress, I have no idea how long it would have taken for them to send me the index card with the number I needed. Maybe the entire process would have taken two months. I don't know because soon after I requested the forms, I found out I could apply for my number online at the Library of Congress Web site (www.loc.gov). I did and received it via email in a matter of hours! So Internet time is really nothing more than how long a process ideally should have taken in the first place.

Discourse and the Shaping of Content

The Internet not only encourages and speeds up discourse, it enables discourse to shape content before the content is even published. Before one of my favorite *Star Trek* reviewers on the Web (www.treknews.com/deltablues/) writes one of his *Star Trek* TV or movie reviews, he is bombarded with emails from people like me who have read his previous reviews, know he's writing another one, and want to get an opinion voiced. Every once in a while, I see something I've sent to him appear in his reviews. And of course people email him to agree or disagree with the review itself. But the point is, our voices are being heard, often before he even writes his review, so the content of the review is modified as it is being created.

Sometimes the shaping of content by discourse is encouraged, as in the case of my *Star Trek* reviewer. Other times, it is not. Often the most intriguing and useful dialog occurs when a text or idea sees the light of day against its author's wishes. The Internet allows anyone to impose the Socratic Dialog, even if it is not wanted. For example, a number of political activists in non-governmental organizations (NGOs) have become experts at ferreting out the details of economic agreements, particularly those relating to globalization. Such agreements are often struck behind closed doors by the economic ministries of various countries. By "liberating" the details of such agreements, NGOs introduce an unwanted but usually necessary level of dialog and transparency to the process, thereby allowing affected parties to have a chance to modify the terms of the agreements before they are finalized. Email, discussion lists, and the Web have been potent weapons in such undertakings, interjecting the Socratic Dialog into global governance as well as many other arenas. This has helped to ensure the transparency of these crucial processes, often against the will of those involved.

Sharing and Amplifying Intellectual Capital

Writing allows ideas to flower. In *The History and Power of Writing*, Henri-Jean Martin says that "writing casts speech onto a two-dimensional space and fixes it there, thus permitting speech to be an object of reflection outside of any context. Furthermore, because it visualizes discourse, writing prompts new sorts of connections in the reasoning process."

The Internet allows writing to move anywhere, at the speed of light, enabling the involvement of a wide variety of people in the flowering of ideas. Having complex documents, plans, proposals, treaties, agreements, standards and even source code circulated among interested parties for the express purpose of generating dialog allows participants to review both the context and the details for coherence and completeness. As a result, the accumulation of robust knowledge within an informed community becomes much greater. Nothing improves quality better than thousands of knowledgeable eyeballs scrutinizing every detail. Furthermore, the evolution toward quality is much quicker because of the speed with which interested parties can communicate.

Once a body of knowledge is formulated, it can then be shared.

The almost infinite shelf space of the Web combines with hypertext and such tools as streaming video webcasts, threaded discussion groups, and instant messaging to provide a rich platform for the transfer of knowledge to anyplace on the globe.

We all like to talk. The Internet gives us a splendid mechanism to hold an enriched conversation with anyone, anywhere on the planet, which no doubt accounts for its incredible growth and popularity. And talk is good. The more we converse, the more we can learn, and the more we learn the more we can contribute. And when people on the Internet start talking, they do what people have always done when they talk – they form communities.

Formation of Community

IT'S GOT AWESOME high-end audio and perfect 3D video. It's fully tactile and in it you can taste and smell anything that is at hand. It's – reality!

Reality gives us the best presence of all, the actual experience of and ability to interact with another person, place, or thing. But due to the constraints imposed by that same reality, we only get to occupy one tiny corner of life at a time – our own personal intersection of the space-time continuum. So until we overcome that minor hurdle, we have to communicate over distance and time with the paler forms of presence that writing and other media allow.

People who love Mozart, people who watch *Star Trek*, corporations that manufacture components for the aerospace industry, pregnant women who will give birth in December, kids with diabetes, authors of fan fiction, sports fanatics, band groupies, and people in countless other communities interact on the Internet every day. Far from being a force for social isolation, for people of like minds or similar interests, the Internet is a wellspring of community formation. Since people who communicate over the Internet usually do so over some distance, they may not get the chance to meet in person. When that's the case, their communication is limited to the exchange of words and pictures and will stay that way until we start beaming ourselves around the planet as fast as we can beam our information today. In the meantime, that portion of our presence that we choose to convey via our correspondence can be as trivial or as rich as we make it.

Conveying Presence

The movie *84 Charing Cross Road*, starring Anne Bancroft and Anthony Hopkins, tells the story of such a relationship, one that flowered via the exchange of letters. Based upon the memoirs of a New York television writer, the movie tells the story of her twenty-year friendship with a London bookseller. It was a friendship that meant a great deal to each of them and blossomed into real affection. Had the characters carried on their correspondence in the late 1990s rather than the 1950s and 1960s, the correspondence no doubt would have been via email. Would the relationship have been better if it could have been face-to-face? Probably. But without the mail, "e" or otherwise, it wouldn't have happened at all. And that's the point. For the characters played by Anne Bancroft and Anthony Hopkins, correspondence enabled the relationship, just like email and the Web do today. They enable conversation, relationship, and the formation of community.

Howard Rheingold (www.rheingold.com), early online pioneer, says this about virtual communities: "I have participated in a wide-ranging, intellectually stimulating, professionally rewarding, sometimes painful, and often intensely emotional ongoing interchange with dozens of new friends, hundreds of colleagues, thousands of acquaintances. And I still spend many of my days in a room, physically isolated. My mind, however, is linked with a worldwide collection of like-minded (and not so like-minded) souls: My virtual community."

If I joined a neighborhood book club, we would meet periodically to discuss the books we've read and share our opinions and insights. The people in the club, however, would be limited to those who were both interested in such an undertaking and who happened to live in the neighborhood. If I joined a book club on the Internet, we would not be able to meet in person but we could still share our opinions and insights. Membership would be limited to those who were interested, but they could live anywhere on the planet, giving the book club a much richer ground from which dialog could grow. The conversations would lack the aspect of physical presence but they would be greatly enriched by the number and diversity of the people who could participate.

Compatriots are not that easy to come by; the hunger for a community of kindred spirits is not always sated by the people who happen to live close. The Internet allows the creation of communities of common interest rather than common location, regardless of how few or many participate, or by how widely they are separated.

Reaching the Niche Audience

As Robert Reid says in *Architects of the Web*, "When audiences are small, dispersed, and anonymous . . . they can rarely be reached economically. In such cases, content is all too often denied an audience, and information consumers are denied access to content."

On the Web, no matter how small the community, if someone develops a site, the few souls who have an interest in it can find it. Furthermore, content can be precisely shaped. Since the size of the audience doesn't determine access, there is no need to appeal to a common taste or to let the message of a site be constrained by the need to please a mass audience. A site can be as arcane, focused, cool, boring, or silly as it needs to be. And once content is on the Internet, a person's interest in it and a search engine become the means of distribution; interest drives distribution because interest drives visits. Best of all, once we get there we're primed to pay attention because we sought it out ourselves.

A Small Corner of Cyberspace

I'm not in an Internet book club, but I'm in something similar – a virtual community of people who email each other after the latest *Star Trek* episode. I met most of my email buddies through their responses to a few rants I posted on the Web; something must have resonated sufficiently with them to prompt an email and start a correspondence. I have never met my *Trek* email buddies in person, even though some have met each other. But that doesn't stop us from having some quite visceral discussions covering the portrayal of women, the rightness or wrongness of the ethics manifested in the episode (ethics is a big topic among Trek-lovers), the consistency of character portrayal and story arc, and the sharing of fiction offerings (since obviously we think we can do it better than the episode writers).

When the season is in full swing, I often think while watching the episode how various of us will react; the thought of the upcoming explication is often more entertaining than the show itself. Correspondence, like interest in anything, waxes and wanes. Nevertheless, through the season and seasons, getting an email from any of them is as delightful as spotting an old friend strolling down the street.

Victorian Email

Relationships formed via correspondence may not always be as multifaceted as they are in real life but they can have a great depth and focus. The medium of email, as opposed to conversation or even instant messaging, allows us time to reflect and compose, making dialog as personal and insightful as we choose. There is a very satisfying quaintness about dealing with people only through the written word; it allows a stately progression of intimacy or no progression at all. The Victorians got some things right and one of them was the exercise of formality in human relations, at least until such a time as the people involved chose to make it otherwise. Ironically, even though it is a modern tool, email can still be quite formal, its nature determined by the fact that it is conveying the written word. The "e" in email just makes the correspondence go further and faster.

Enhancing Physical Communities

We can use the Internet to bridge distance. We can also use it to make our local community experience more rich, diverse, and interesting by enabling conversations between people who live close or already know one another. People in communities such as schools and neighborhoods can strengthen their existing bonds through the Internet's ability to enable conversation. In fact many neighborhoods are beginning to create Web sites to link people together, enable commerce, discuss civic issues, and generally increase the flow of information in and through the community. Imagine having a Web site for your neighborhood through which you could order a pizza, get an email when ice cream goes on sale, check school closings, view restaurant menus, review school homework assignments, sign up for programs at the park, reserve a book at the library, ventilate on a current community issue, start an email campaign to get a pothole fixed, view the new art at the local gallery, find a kid to cut the grass, and send out a community alert.

Much interaction on the Internet is in fact local and definitely not anonymous, especially for younger participants, who have to face the results of their chats the next day in school when their friends come armed with printed transcripts. And often people who meet online eventually meet in real life, with the added twist of already knowing a lot about each other. So rather than meeting and getting to know a person, you get to know them first and *then* meet them. Real life enhances cyber-relationships!

The Virtual Corporation

In one of the writing jobs I had recently, gained via my Web site, my client was a small "rent-a-programmer" company. This one-man company was putting together a team for a software development for the financial division of a large auto maker. It turned out that, like our team, the entire software development staff – including managers – actually worked for someone else, and came together just for this project. Some worked on site, some worked at home. Everyone was on everyone else's instant messaging "buddy" list and we could communicate with each other regardless of location. The development was well managed, using state-of-the-art tools and formal methodologies. But no one on the team was an employee of the corporation, except the senior vice president responsible for the project.

The Internet easily enables this sort of ad hoc organization, bringing together people on a project basis rather than in a traditional employer-employee relationship. It has the potential, for folks in some types of jobs anyway, to make us all free-lancers, negotiating each project as it comes. The only thing that wasn't virtual were the people involved, the work product, and the check in my mailbox at the end of the week.

The Internet dissolves barriers, the main but not the only one being distance, and provides a forum for conversation, debate, and interaction. It links people of common interests who would not otherwise have met and gives a voice to some people who might not otherwise have one. Just like life, the bigger and more complex the Internet gets, the more differentiated it becomes and the more unique. The same goes (on a good day) for the individuals and communities that use it.

GETTING THE WEB

The Community that Created the Internet

The Internet itself is the product of such a complex and differentiated community. The Internet owes its existence and continuing health to a community of cooperation that was formed on it, consisting of those people who participate in the Requests for Comments (RFC) process (www.rfc-editor.org). The Internet isn't "run" by any one central organization. It works because the people involved have all argued about and agreed upon the open standards and procedures that make it work, via submitting and commenting upon RFCs. There are more than 2800 RFCs to date, covering Internet open standards specifications as well as "networking protocols, procedures, programs, and concepts but also including meeting notes, opinion, and sometimes humor" (www.rfc-editor.org/overview.html). Anyone can submit a draft RFC for publication; if it survives the review process, it becomes a part of the official documentation of the Internet. RFC documents hold the technical history of the Internet; the community that continues to write RFCs holds its future evolution. Membership in this community is open to anyone who has the technical expertise, desire, and commitment to participate.

Doing Good and Showing Off

On the Internet, it's not unusual for people who would otherwise be complete strangers to do cool stuff as a community for no other reason than their love of doing cool stuff. The Internet has a very strong culture of gifts, inherited from its scientific beginnings. In the Internet's culture of gifts, people often contribute just because they want to, to give back to the Web, to gain visibility and fame, and to take advantage of peer review. Reflecting this culture, many successful businesses on the Web give something away. For example, the lite version of a software application might be free or the client in a client/server product.

People getting together to do cool stuff grew the Internet and the Web. It also created the open source movement, a quite complex and definitely differentiated community, and its child, the Linux operating system.

Open Source

The open source movement takes the "open" approach that we've seen applied to standards (i.e., published, owned by no one, used by all) and applies it to source code, the words that contain the human-readable logic of computer software. All proponents of open source say that source code should be published for all to see, to comment upon, to debug and enhance. And in fact, many of the key software tools used on the Web today have some or all of their source code published, including the Linux operating system, the Netscape browser, the Perl programming language, and the Apache Web server, the software that powers more than half the servers on the Web. Some proponents of open source go further and say that source code should be possessed by no one and usable by all, meaning that you could not only look at it, but change it, redistribute it, and even sell it, as long as you give your customer the same rights. "To understand the concept, you should think of free speech, not free beer," says Richard Stallman, pioneer of the free software movement.

The free software movement (www.gnu.org) has even drafted its own copyright license – which they refer to as a "copyleft" (www.gnu.org/copyleft/gpl.html). It is the GNU General Public License and it comes with free GNU software to insure that it stays free. The license states that you can use the free software to make more software of your own, but you cannot put any restrictions on its use, which gets to the point of free speech vs. free beer. For example, if you use free software to make a software application, you can sell that software to your customers, but you can't restrict your customers from changing it or selling it again if they so choose. It's an interesting way to insure that a gift remains a gift. Even more interestingly, a similar license exists for text. It may seem ironic to have copyright language protecting a gift, but it ultimately makes sense. Strong copyright laws can both protect the content by which people choose to make a living as well as ensuring that what they give back to the Web stays free.

Open source is also pushing software to change from a product to a service. Rather than being delivered as a proprietary, shrink-wrapped, manufactured object, software is being delivered as a part of a service that also includes customization, training, and support. So it just goes to prove that on the Internet, you can give stuff away and still make a buck!

Transparency and Complexity

Linux, an open source operating system, is an incredibly complex piece of software. It is also incredibly robust and stable, since its insides have been published and scrutinized by countless educated eyeballs. The transparency manifested by the open source movement is a concept that would do well to travel to other industries. Wouldn't you feel safer knowing that all the engineering diagrams and maintenance procedures of the jumbo jet upon which you and your loved ones are flying had been scrutinized by an army of independent engineers? At some point, as both shareholders and customers, we will have to decide which is more important, the proprietary nature of a design or its quality. Obviously both are important, but today, for most designs of any complexity, their proprietary nature comes first. Thanks to the transparency we're getting used to on the Web, that may not always be the case. By its support of such transparency, the Internet may have given us just the antidote we need to the ever-increasing complexities of daily life. Not bad work for a bunch of strangers in a virtual community getting together to do cool stuff.

FORMATION OF COMMUNITY

Cyberspace is Earth

If you spend hours on the phone at work, you don't come home and say, "I spent the day in phonespace." If you curl up and loose yourself with a great book on a rainy weekend, you don't report to your friends on Monday that you spent the weekend in "bookspace." They in turn don't worry that you are "cutting yourself off from the human community." You automatically know that when you talk on the phone or read a book, you are taking advantage of a tool that enables a special kind of communication that often, especially with books, can be of the highest order. Telephones and books are blissfully free of the technological blather often attached to "cyberspace."

Because it is so pervasive and so new, it is easy to view the Web as having no context, as existing as a self-contained universe unto itself. In reality, of course, that view is a bit balmy. Just like every book in existence was written and published by a set of humans for purposes of communication and exchange, every Web site in "cyberspace" is written and served by a set of humans for the same reasons.

This fact was brought home to me in a happy way when I attended a seminar put on by the Publishers Marketing Association. Up to that point, I had approached my adventure into publishing almost exclusively via books and the Web. I had surfed countless Web sites, bought books on the Web about publishing, and struck up email correspondences with a number of folks who had been very helpful. But I have to admit, it was great to see all the faces of all the people whose books and words I've been reading. Everyone was so delightfully – well, so delightfully human. When it came time to plunk down the thousands of dollars required to print a book, I did so because seeing all those people proved what I already knew, if only intellectually. There really are humans behind all those Web sites! Even a company as "cyber" as Amazon is in business today not only because of its Web site, but because of the thousands of people all over the country and world who pull physical books off physical shelves in physical warehouses and see that the books get wrapped and shipped via snail-mail to the right mailboxes on our doorsteps.

The Internet is a tool of communication and exchange so the humans behind the communications and the exchanges ultimately determine the course of events. When I converse with a potential client online, earthly concerns dominate. Is this person rational? Can we work together to create a good product? Will I get paid? Likewise, the client wants to know if I'm honest and competent and if I'll deliver a good product in a timely fashion. The fact that we wiggle bits on each other's screens to communicate in no way diminishes the importance of these concerns. When you enter "cyberspace" you bring your humanity, your self-interest, and your morals with you and those more than anything determine the success or failure of your interaction. And there's nothing virtual about that.

There's also nothing virtual about the changes that will occur when individuals all over the planet can carry on enriched conversations and form communities with whomever they choose. Institutions can't help but change when information flows freely, when anyone can publish, when barriers to entry for many businesses are virtually eliminated, when intellectual capital increases, when feedback shapes content, when communities of interest gain voice, when local communities thrive, and when complex and differentiated entities form and emerge like the open source movement and the Internet itself.

Individuals in conversation and community are driving the changes we're seeing so far and will continue to generate change for some time to come.

Conversations Driving Change

THE INTERNET doesn't cause change but the people using it certainly do. If there are conversations between people and within communities that the Internet can bring about, it is from these conversations that change will come. My intent is not to predict such changes but to show that they are not only predictable but often obvious when seen from the perspective of what can happen when individuals and organizations can talk directly to one another. Conversations enabled by the Internet will drive structural shifts in the way we do things, creating new institutions, evolving some, and evaporating others.

Webster's College Dictionary defines capitalism as follows: "an economic system in which investment in and ownership of the means of production, distribution, and the exchange of wealth is made and maintained chiefly by private individuals or corporations." Besides making us all publishers, the Web can make us all capitalists. And since capitalism has often been described as "creative destruction," some of us will be in for quite a ride.

The free flow of words, pictures, sound, motion, and logic on the Internet will make obvious new ways of doing things. When people have information and global access, institutions can't help but change. If your mission, business, or joy in life can be affected by a communication or an exchange, look for transformation. Then figure out how to ride the swell and maybe even grab the rudder and the sail.

The Free Flow of Information

In billions of Web pages and emails, there is a tremendous amount of information zipping around the planet every day. Traffic on the Internet follows the Sun, with traffic peaks generated by morning in Australia, Japan and other places in the Far East. They are followed by additional peaks as day dawns in Europe and a few hours later in the Americas. You have to figure that at least some of this information is more than idle chatter, that some of it is getting absorbed by the people having all these conversations and that it is making a difference.

The book you hold exists because of the Internet, first of all and most obviously because it is about the Internet and the Web. But equally as important, the information available on the Web and the conversations I was able to have enabled both its research and writing, and more critically, its publication. I had access to a world of information about publishing, including books that were available and annotated online that would otherwise have been unknown or inaccessible. I had direct access to organizations and corporations who play key roles in book publishing. Want to get an ISBN number for your book and get listed in Books In Print? Apply online at www.bowker.com. How about a Library of Congress Control Number, so libraries can buy your book? Apply online at www.loc.gov. To get your book with the two major wholesalers in the United States, go to their Web sites at www.btol.com and www.ingrambookgroup.com. Want to see how much it will cost to get your book printed? Fill out the online quote form at any of the forty or so book printers in the United States. And to help you market your book, go to the Publishers Marketing Association at www.pma-online.org. Along with all this information, I had access to people in the industry via email, most of whom were kind enough to answer the dumb questions of a complete stranger. I could therefore get the big picture of what needed to be done, get detailed information when I needed it, and most importantly get the confidence I needed at each step of the way to move on to the next step.

New worlds can open up to anyone who takes the time to track down the information they require and to ask the questions they need answered. Information for the most part is no longer held only in corporate methods and procedures or hidden in the dark recesses of local area networks. It is hung out on the Web for all to see; information and access have become both democratic and global.

Access Changes Structure

The fact that individuals and organizations across the globe can deal directly with each other is bound to cause some "creative destruction." Here's one example of a considerable change that a simple online transaction can generate.

Many of us buy books online and Amazon.com is a popular retailer. Amazon sells books in the United States and also has sites in other countries, including one in the United Kingdom. When the wildly popular Harry Potter fantasy books came out, they topped the best seller lists at both sites. And when one of the books appeared months earlier in the U.K. than it did in the States, eager American customers simply ordered the book online from Amazon U.K. If you wanted the book, it was a completely sensible thing to do. But it created a fuss in the publishing industries in both countries, because both industries are built on separate rights structures. To get a book published in the United States, an author typically assigns the "North American rights" for the book to an American publisher. However, if that book is sold in America by a British publisher, are those rights violated? If you buy a book from a site in the U.K. using a computer in the United States, where is the book "sold?" The selling of foreign rights by publishers to other publishers is a big, complex business. It is also one that will inevitably be restructured, for the simple reason that now people can buy books with ease from anywhere they want, making geographical grants of rights increasingly obsolete. We don't have "Indiana rights," or "North Dakota" rights; one day "North American rights" will seem equally peculiar. And this is just one example of how global access generates structural change.

Here's another example of structural change caused by global access and the Internet's ability to quickly and freely copy huge quantities of information. If folks can do something, they generally will, and they are using the MP3 audio standard to produce and share music files in many creative ways, some considered illegal. Existing copyright laws did a great job when no one had the ability to make a digital copy of a song, but now everybody can. It doesn't take much to convert a CD to MP3 format and post it on a Web site; some sites have already purchased and digitized tens of thousands of CDs. Sites like Napster also exist to enable the online trading of MP3 files by individuals. The recording industry may come to terms in court with individual companies such as Napster. However, people using the underlying technology will continue to do so and drive changes to which the industry will have to adjust.

The Internet, multinational corporations, and the international standards committees are all global. The World Trade Organization, the World Bank, the International Monetary Fund, and the thousands of non-governmental organizations often opposing them and "liberating" their texts are also all global. Global organizations are often the real forces that will shape the institutional structures of the future. But most of the institutions we know today are still defined by national boundaries. Clearly this will lead to all kinds of challenging "growth experiences" in the years to come as global communication and exchange prompts shifts in existing bounded structures.

Everyone's an Operator

With information and access becoming democratic and global, everyone becomes an "operator." In the old days, you needed a telephone operator to place your telephone call. Later, you could dial local calls yourself but needed an operator to dial your long distance calls. Now you can dial local, domestic, and international long distance calls yourself; you are your own operator. Soon you will become your own customer service representative. In the old days, customers talked over the phone to customer representatives who worked with paper records. Corporations computerized the records but customers still had to call to transact business. Now, you can start to deal directly with corporate and organizational sites on the Web and manipulate and control your own digital records in order to get information or execute your transactions.

You can also become your own sales representative. Many computer companies like Apple and Dell have online stores that allow customers to select various attributes of the computers they are buying (e.g., RAM, hard disk size, monitor type, cards, etc.); the machines are then made to order. More and more corporations are dealing with both customers and suppliers directly via the Web by creating complex, online interfaces through which business is transacted. Who knows, maybe one day we won't even need online stock brokers because we'll all have our own virtual seats on a global stock exchange!

The Price in the Marketplace

In a marketplace, the buyer looks for the lowest price and the seller tries for the highest price. If the seller is more eager than the buyer, the price will drop. If the buyer is more eager, the price will rise. But what happens if the conversation suddenly becomes global? If I am buying baseball cards or Beanie Babies locally in Chicago, the price I am willing to pay is determined both by my eagerness as well as by what's available in that particular market. I may not really want to pay the stated price for Bessie the Cow or a 1959 White Sox card, but if I'm eager, I just might. On the other hand, if I find the same items on a Web site in Boston for less, I'll make the purchase there. The Internet makes it easier for everyone to know what everyone else is buying, selling, and paying. This free flow of information causes prices to level out, allowing supply and demand to function more effectively in a much broader arena. Price is no longer bounded by the size of the market because the market is global.

Some sites such as Priceline.com go even further in using information to affect price. They allow individuals to do on the Web what they are unable to do in person – band together to get a volume discount. On such sites, the more people that agree to buy a particular item, the lower the price; the site effectively serves to negotiate a discount based on volume. Such sites allow people to use the power of group buying to generate savings. People get a better price, sellers get customers they might not otherwise have gotten, and of course the site takes a slice off the top of every transaction.

The Marketplace Itself

The Internet allows you to participate in many new markets; it also allows you to create markets yourself. After all, a market is simply the place where a buyer meets a seller to complete an exchange. Individuals, communities, corporations and whole industries are figuring out that they can create marketplaces of their own to connect buyers and sellers quite efficiently, providing a place to get the best product or service for the best price. This works not only for customer-to-customer transactions, but also for business-to-business transactions. Many of the new business-to-business e-commerce enterprises are just such sites, creating for specific industries a place for buyers and sellers to get together; some even mediate business-to-business barter.

A Market of One

When I shop at Amazon.com, Amazon says hello. It greets me by name, offers recommendations in books and music and fires up that tempting "One Click" button. When I look at a book, Amazon shows me reviews by professionals as well as ordinary individuals (sometimes less diplomatic) who have also read the book. It also tells me what related books people have purchased. And it does this more than a million times a day, for most all of the visitors it gets. Even if it is done via computer, Amazon recognizes that its customers are individuals and not part of some faceless "mass market."

Such Internet experiences may very well generate a psychological shift in the way consumers behave. "Consumers" have traditionally been seen as passive absorbers who respond or don't respond to a general message pushed to a mass market. But once an individual gets on the Web, the next online store is only a click away, so it is much harder for the seller to hold the buyer and complete the transaction. This creates leverage for the buyer and helps to generate higher levels of service and personalization.

This is what Christopher Locke says about online markets in *The Cluetrain Manifesto*:

> Companies that are actually communicating with online markets have flung the doors wide open. They're constantly searching for solid information they can share with customers and prospects via Web and FTP sites, email lists, phone calls, whatever it takes. They're not half as concerned with protecting their data as with

how much information they can give away. That's how they stay in touch, stay competitive, keep market attention from drifting to competitors. Such companies are creating a new kind of corporate identity, based not on the repetitive advertising needed to create 'brand awareness,' but on substantive, personalized communications.

The Internet is generating big changes in those areas of society touched by communication and exchange because it gives voice to individuals and communities and makes information and access global. Successful businesses on the Internet have already figured this out. They know that their ultimate customer is an individual able to engage in a global conversation and empowered with a voice (and a mouse). Such businesses succeed by recognizing that the individual defines the context of the encounter, not the business.

These businesses have been at the forefront of Internet-driven change, as have the individuals they cater to. The great part comes when such individuals start to figure out just how backward and dense other institutions are in comparison. Amazon has spoiled us, and that is a good thing. We should expect to be recognized first and foremost as individuals by all of the institutions that claim to serve us. (Now quit laughing!) Fortunately, the more empowered we are, the more we will be able to reward the institutions that get it and wallop the ones that don't.

The Internet may be just the thing we need to permanently nail into place the mother of all paradigm shifts: the idea that the person gives meaning to the institution, not the other way around. If the individuals who use the Internet can serve to make this simple fact that much more obvious, they will make the world a saner place.

An Outbreak of Sanity

THE OCEAN LINER Titanic went down mainly due to cockiness, but even given the astounding arrogance of the times, had the White Star Line and the captain been able to know in sufficient detail the location of that iceberg, they could have avoided hitting it.

The world is often said to be shrinking. But at the same time, it's getting grander and richer and more complex and more surprising. The Internet and the Web can help us cope with this increasing abundance and complexity by giving us the information we need to become more aware and get a better grip. The more varied the sources of information we have, the more we can create a better map of reality in which to operate and grow. Complexity can be good; it is the stuff of life. It differentiates, making us more distinctly ourselves. Tielhard de Chardin says in *The Phenomenon of Man* that: "At each further degree of combination, something which is irreducible to isolated elements emerges in a new order." (New York: Harper & Row, 1959).

It's just like *Star Trek's* Vulcan philosophy: "Infinite Diversity in Infinite Combinations." Gene Roddenberry invented the world of *Star Trek* in a pre-Internet Earth. In the future he envisioned, chaos and destruction ruled the world until the year 2063, when the Vulcans, with their wonderful philosophy and technology, came to visit. Things cheered up on Earth after that. But maybe if Roddenberry had been writing in a world connected by the Web, he would have envisioned a happier Earth before the Vulcans got here.

The free flow of information also helps to reduce the illusions and delusions that generate so much fear and hate. The telephone company for computers enables us to have enriched conversations and a planet in conversation is much more apt to work things out than to blow itself to smithereens.

Illumination and Formalization

The Internet, being the offspring of computers and telephones, has inherited a very important characteristic from the computer side of its family tree. Computer systems analysis and design principles tell us that when you computerize a manual procedure, you first must lay out all the steps of the procedure to see which parts are amenable to computerization. This means that you have to throw light on the entire routine, writing it all down, and permitting it to named, recorded, and reflected upon. Once it's written down, you can look at it, turn it around, prod it and poke it, make new connections, and determine how you ultimately want things to work.

Computerizing a process serves to illuminate and formalize it, which can be occasionally embarrassing if it happens to be illogical or if it involves nefarious behavior (e.g., "Okay, this is the point in the process where I usually take the bribe . . . Oops"). Computerizing a process also inhibits arbitrariness, again because all the logic has to be written down for the computer to do its job. It makes it difficult to swipe money, put in the fix, grant the building permit to your cousin for free, or yank the passport application of someone whose politics you don't happen to like.

Any bureaucracy where corruption thrives isn't going to like getting its procedures computerized and will like even less having them computerized and hung out on the Web for all to see. Computerization and the Internet help move control from the arbitrary will of a person to a transparent, knowable process, like the historical progression from the rule of caesars and kings to the rule of law.

Illuminating and formalizing the bureaucratic process, as well as restricting its arbitrariness, helps to augment one of the themes of the Internet era – transparency.

Transparency

Transparency involves surrender of control to a visible process. If something is transparent, anyone can see into it, can know it and can know how it works. Laws, standards, treaties, agreements, methods, procedures, and just about anything else that people negotiate can be made transparent.

- In countries run by the rule of law, laws are both formal and transparent. They are published for all to see so people know what is and what is not legal. Anyone can walk into any courtroom and watch any proceeding. However, in totalitarian regimes, the law is arbitrary and shrouded. You can get hauled off to jail in the middle of the night without recourse for breaking a "law" you have never heard of.
- Open standards are transparent; proprietary standards are not. For example, the MP3 standard is transparent. The International Standards Organization has published a technical specification of MP3 so anyone can write client software or server software for MP3 files. On the other hand, the RealAudio standard is not transparent. Its internal workings are not open to public view or use and its evolution is controlled solely by RealNetworks.
- Open source is transparent. The source code for the

Linux operating system has been published for all to see and its insides have been scrutinized by countless educated eyeballs, resulting in a product that is incredibly robust and stable. Microsoft's Windows operating system is not transparent. Microsoft considers the source code of Windows to be its intellectual property so its insides (including any flaws and redundancies) are hidden.

❐ In the United States, accounting practices are transparent. Businesses adhere to the generally accepted accounting principles defined by the Financial Accounting Standards Board and have their financial reports prepared by external auditors. Other countries, depending upon their level of development and openness, have their own standards or adhere to those set forth by the International Accounting Standards Committee.

Transparency is a critical attribute of systems and processes because it puts them out in the open where they can be analyzed and reflected upon. When you're dealing with something that is transparent, you know what you're getting. Because you can see into it, you know how to use it, you can judge what comes out of it, and you have a means to cope if something goes wrong. Writing has always been a means to authenticate, serving to establish the reality of commercial transactions (e.g., "You owe me 40 oxen, not 20, and I have the tablets to prove it!"). Writing words and logic for the Web extends that transparency and delivers predictability, authentication, and accountability to all involved. Even kids in chat rooms and online conversations have figured this out. If something particularly important or juicy is said, they often print it out, save it, and pass it around as evidence the next day in school: They make their chats transparent.

Corruption is one of the major banes of modern existence

and transparency is a potent antidote. As Thomas Friedman says in *The Lexus and the Olive Tree*, "There is no greater restraint on human behavior than having other people watching exactly what you're up to." Political activists in non-governmental organizations have taken this approach, "liberating" the details of economic agreements to force transparency and dialog.

We may all be surprised when accountants waving Financial Accounting Standards Board bulletins are hailed as the heroes and heroines of the new, transparent world order, sending corrupt officials slinking off into the night. After all, accountants invented writing; ridding the world of corruption would make a nice encore!

We have seen with Linux and the open source movement the power of transparency when it comes to managing complexity in software such as operating systems. If complex entities are transparent, communities of knowledge on the Internet will be able to scrutinize and evolve them to the point where they perform precisely and consistently. It seems to me that Linux signifies complexity with transparency while Windows signifies complexity without transparency; there is no contest between the two when it comes to stability and robustness. Transparency is one big reason why.

The Internet nourishes the practice of transparency in two ways. First, because the Internet itself is transparent, since it is based on open standards. Second, because illumination and formalization occur when processes are computerized. Anywhere on the globe that the Internet goes, transparency has a good chance of following.

Epiphanies of Context

With increased information, formalization and transparency, it's easier to get a clearer picture of reality. Our global conversations, as well as the billion or so pages on the Web, form a wealth of varied, concrete, and detailed evidence showing us what the world is like. This evidence makes it tougher to be oblivious and makes our awareness of each other stronger, wider, richer, and deeper. And once our awareness expands, we are apt to see and do things differently. This happens because a widening awareness expands the context in which we see, changing the framework of meaning.

What a standard does for a string of bits, context does for reality – it gives us a framework of meaning. Logic works great once the inputs are defined, but you need context to frame the issue. Context answers the question, "What's this ultimately about?" It defines the big picture, created from our recognition of the world around us. Increasing awareness expands the context, changing the framework of meaning.

Here's an example. If you buy stock in a corporation, you want the stock to go up so you can get a good return on your investment. However, as a good citizen, you want the corporation run in a legal and responsible manner – no graft, no corruption, no unfair labor practices. Your desire to have a good return on your investment easily lives within the higher context of responsible corporate behavior. Now let's say that while your corporation is a good citizen in the United States, in other countries it has engaged in corrupt practices and maximized your shareholder value through the use of child labor. If you know nothing of such practices, you have no problem. However, once you find out, you realize that the return on your investment is brought to you through corruption and the exploitation of children. Once you know, you can't help but see your investment in a different context. Your investment used to be just about money; now it's about money and exploitation. Its meaning changes, as does your responsibility. You must now judge how best to respond as an investor (and therefore part owner) of the company.

Let's take another example. Suppose that you are a shareholder in an airline. You are also, like many shareholders, a customer of the airline. So the needs of the shareholder and the needs of the customer come together in one person and that person is you. So you ask the question, "What is a good airline ultimately about?" And since you are an Internet-empowered individual, able to form community with other shareholders, customers, and employees to make your voice heard, you and your community just might form a consensus *on your own terms* of what a good airline is ultimately about. You therefore might be able to make a difference by creating a new context – a context that changes what it means to "maximize shareholder value." Such new meaning might evolve into a more transparent way of running the corporation, in which shareholders more fully scrutinize management practices, decisions and plans.

Our use of the Internet may end up changing us the most because it expands our knowledge of reality, giving us new ways to frame issues.

Increasing awareness also increases responsibility and gives us less excuse to behave badly out of ignorance. The well-known logo on the Apple computer – the bitten apple – is no small symbol of the age in which we live.

Once you take that bite from the fruit of the tree of knowledge, you must deal one way or another with that knowledge. You can't behave responsibly about something if you are unaware of it. On the other hand, once you become aware, you are obligated by that very awareness to act on that knowledge. By increasing awareness, the Internet acts to expand and deepen the context in which we see each other and gives us the opportunity to behave in a more ethical fashion.

Welcome to the Renaissance

The hallmark of the Renaissance that started in Fourteenth and Fifteenth Century Florence was the primacy of the individual.

If many of us feel an affinity for that time, it may be because we sense that it's up to us to proceed with what the Renaissance started.

In a sane world, individuals create the ultimate context for institutions, not the other way around. Institutions have meaning and worth because they are given meaning by individuals and gain worth through the functions they perform.

Information illuminates. With it, we can see ourselves in the full context of who we really are and insure through transparency that our organizations function the way they should. Using the Internet, each individual, alone or in communities of interest and knowledge, finally has the power to trump the agenda of the institution and shape it to serve those who give it meaning.

Breakthroughs in behavior often occur when enough people simply recognize the same fact as obvious and act accordingly. Individuals in conversation and community will ultimately make it obvious that every person, regardless of circumstance or location on the planet, has the right to develop in to a fully self-realized human being with the responsibility to help others do the same.

"We're all connected but no one's in charge?" Nope. "We're all connected and everyone's in charge!" Humanity emerges from its violent childhood, mouse in hand. One of the uses of conversation and community is the nurturing of rationality. For the first time in history, we have the tools to create not only worldwide health but worldwide sanity. I think we have some sense of what a prosperous and healthy world might look like. But what would a sane world look like? Now there's a topic for an online discussion group! It would not be a perfect world, but it would be a world where people busy themselves solving problems, helping others, self-actualizing, and of course doing cool stuff on the Internet.

Ours will soon be a world in which most individuals on the

planet will be connected via the telephone company for computers and will be able to carry on enriched conversations with anyone they choose. Such a networked world gives anyone with a powerful idea an extraordinary *leverage* to make a difference, particularly within a specific sphere of interest, or community, or industry, or profession. Any individual or community that is looking for a free, diverse, complex, and ever-growing source of conversation about what the world is like will find it on the Web. And any individual or community that is looking for a place to imagine and create the future will find it on the Web.

Come on in. Use your voice. Create a site. Join a conversation. Join a community or form one yourself. Turn on some lights. Change some context. Move your corner of the world.

The Web is yours.

About the Author

Jeanne M. Follman has followed with great interest the growth of the Internet and the Web since going online in 1994. She has been a technology writer for ten years as well as a Web developer, a programmer, and a manager of software development projects. She is a contributor to various publications, including *OnTheInternet*, the official publication of the Internet Society (www.isoc.org). Two chapters of this book (*Files of Words, Content and Connection*) first appeared in the electronic version of this publication. She is also the creator of Wanda Wigglebits (www.wigglebits.com) and her guide to *Building a School Web Site*. She lives in Chicago with her family.

Glossary

Asymmetric Digital Subscriber Line (ADSL) – a technology for bringing broadband Internet access to homes over ordinary copper telephone wires. ADSL is the most familiar of a family of DSL (Digital Subscriber Line) technologies and is referred to as Asymmetric because it is designed to provide quicker downloads than uploads.

Backbone – On the Internet, a set of high-speed communication lines (e.g., T1, T3, optical carriers) that connect other networks and carry network traffic to distant locations. Local and regional networks connect to the Internet backbone via Network Access Points (NAPs) in various locations in the country and the world. For example, an email from Chicago to Washington, D.C. might travel over a local telephone network to the NAP in downtown Chicago, over the backbone to the D.C. area, and then on to its destination via a local network in Washington, D.C.

Bandwidth – a measure of how much information can flow from one place to another in a given amount of time. Bandwidth is a function of both capacity and speed. On the Internet it is purely a matter of capacity since speed is determined by the physics of electricity and light. Capacity, however, depends on the communication line. A high-speed line is fast because it's fat; it allows many bits to march side by side rather than in single file. Therefore more of them reach their destination in the same amount of time. The wider the line, the greater the bandwidth. On the Internet, we measure bandwidth by measuring how many bits can move from one place to another in one second. We call it bits per second, or bps. See Broadband

Bit – a digit in Base 2 with a value of either 0 or 1. All the information on computers and the Internet is encoded using combinations of bits as defined by various standards. For example, here's how you use bits to say "Hello" as encoded using the American Standard Code for Information Interchange (ASCII):

01001000 01100101 01101100 01101100 01101111

Bits can be arranged in files to create digitized representations of just about anything, including words, pictures, sound and motion, and programs.

bps (bits per second) – a measure of bandwidth on the Internet. See Bits, Bandwidth

Broadband – a type of communication line that is high-speed and permanently connected. The high-speed capacity allows more bits to travel side by side rather than in single file so more of them reach their destination in the same amount of time. The always-on nature of the connection means that you do not have to dial into the Internet – you are always connected. The T1 line that connects some schools to the Internet is an example of a broadband connection. Via such technologies as Digital Subscriber Line (DSL) and cable modems, broadband access to the Internet is becoming available to individuals as well as institutions. It will slowly replace dial-up access. See Bandwidth

Browser – a software program that allows you to look at and interact with information on the World Wide Web. Netscape Navigator and Internet Explorer are examples of popular browsers. In the client/server framework, a browser is a client (e.g., a program whose main job is to request and receive information). See Client/Server

Cable TV Internet Access – a technology for bringing broadband Internet access to homes over cable TV lines through the use of a cable modem.

Client/Server – on the Internet, a way to structure software that divides programs into those that send and those that receive. Every communication has a sender, a signal, and a receiver. On the Internet, it's the same:

- Sender – the server – a software program whose function is to present files so they can be obtained by clients.
- Signal – the file – the content of the communication (e.g., files of words, pictures, sound, motion, logic).

GLOSSARY

❏   Receiver – the client – a software program whose function is to obtain files from a distant server and display or play them so they can be seen or heard. For example, a Web browser is a client software program that downloads and displays Web files from all over the planet.

Clients require specific servers and servers expect certain clients; both must agree on the format of the file. A standard defines each specific client/server interaction and file format.

Compression – a technique to reduce the size of a file so that it takes up less space and can be more quickly transmitted.

Dial-up – a means to access the Internet by using a modem to dial into an Internet Service Provider (ISP). The ISP then completes your connection to the Internet. Dial-up access to the Internet will eventually be replaced by broadband access.

Digital Subscriber Line (DSL). See ADSL

Digitize – the process of translating words, pictures, sound, and video into a series of bits so they can be manipulated by a computer and transmitted on the Internet.

Domain Name – that portion of a Web address (i.e., URL) that is used to identify the network address of a server on the Internet. Wigglebits.com is an example of a domain name. The domain name system is the telephone book of the Internet.

Download – the act of obtaining a file from a distant computer (i.e., server).

File – a chunk of bits in a computer that represent words, pictures, sound, video, or logic. On the Internet, each Web page is typically a file, as is each image. See Client/Server

HTML (Hyper Text Markup Language) – an open standard that defines the way in which hypertext Web pages display and are linked to one another. HTML is one of the three open standards – HTML, HTTP and URL – that Tim Berners-Lee wrote, thereby inventing the World Wide Web.

HTTP (Hyper Text Transfer Protocol) – an open standard that defines how files of information move between clients and servers on the Web. HTTP is one of the three open standards – HTML, HTTP and URL –

that Tim Berners-Lee wrote, thereby inventing the World Wide Web.

Hypertext – a mechanism to organize content. Each component of the content can contain a connection (i.e., link) to another component of the content that displays when the link is clicked. The World Wide Web is the most obvious example of hypertext, but there are others. Help files, for example, often use hypertext as the means to present help information.

Internet – a public, worldwide system of computer networks – the telephone company for computers. It is a collection of interconnected networks using the TCP/IP protocol.

Internet Service Provider (ISP) – a company that provides access to the Internet as well as other services such as email, news, and Web site hosting. If your school or organization has its own direct link to the Internet (e.g., a T1 line), it would not need the services of an ISP since it would perform similar services internally.

Link – in hypertext, the connection between one hypertext object (e.g., words, images) and an other. Clicking the link causes the display of the connected hypertext object.

Metadata – information about information. On the Web, it refers to the information contained in a Web site, usable by search engines, that describes the Web site itself, such as its description and keywords.

Modem – a device between your computer and the voice telephone network that translates bits into various tones audible to the network. Newer digital modems used in broadband access manage the transmission of our bits to the Internet in a digital fashion.

Network – a series of communication lines connecting computers and other communications devices. The Internet is a network of networks.

Open Standard – a set of rules, interfaces, or procedures that is agreed upon by those involved so that any object adhering to the standard can interact with any other object adhering to the same standard. An open standard is a published standard that is possessed by no one and used by all. See Proprietary Standard

Optical Carrier – the standards and technology associated with the transmission of information across fiber optic communication lines. These babies are the fastest (i.e., widest) of the broadband communication

GLOSSARY

lines available today, allowing bits to travel at speeds of over 13 billion bps.

Packet – a piece of a file. When files travel across the Internet, they are broken into chunks called packets. Each packet contains an identification and the address of where it is going. When the packets arrive at their destination, they are reassembled into a file and displayed in a browser. See TCP/IP

Pixel – a dot of color on a computer monitor. The color in the dot is defined by some combination of red, green, and blue. The more bits you use to define how much of each color the dot contains, the greater the range of color the dot can have.

Plug-in – a software program that acts as a client and is integrated into a browser rather than being launched separately.

Proprietary Standard – a set of rules, interfaces, or procedures that exists so that any object adhering to the standard can interact with any other object adhering to the same standard. A proprietary standard is typically owned by a corporation. Its internals cannot be inspected. Its use is licensed by its owners. It can be changed at will. See Open Standard

Pull – a means of communication in which the receiver controls the nature, timing and extent of a communication. Web surfing is an example of *Pull*.

Push – a means of communication that delivers information to the user rather than waiting for the user to specifically request it. In *Push*, the nature and timing of the communication is controlled by the sender. Junk mail is an example of *Push*.

Server – see Client/Server

Streaming – a technique for downloading an audio or video file that allows the client to start playing the file while it is still being transmitted. The client and server work together to manage the transmission, play the file as it downolads, and keep the playing smooth despite network traffic.

T1, T3 – broadband communication lines that carry information at around 1.5 and 45 million bps.

GETTING THE WEB

TCP/IP (Transmission Control Protocol / Internet Protocol) – an open standard that defines how files are broken into packets, routed across the Internet, and put back together again at their destination. The Transmission Control Protocol (TCP) layer of TCP/IP manages the disassembling and reassembling of files and packets and the Internet Protocol (IP) layer gets them to where they belong.

URL (Uniform Resource Locator) – an open standard originally written by Tim Berners-Lee that defines how information in files is located on the Web. The URL identifies both the location of the server on the Internet as well as the location of the files within the folders on the server. URL is one of the three open standards – HTML, HTTP and URL – that Tim Berners-Lee wrote, thereby inventing the World Wide Web.

Web, WWW (World Wide Web) – the "clickable" part of the Internet accessible via a browser. Tim Berners-Lee invented the World Wide Web by writing three open standards – HTML, HTTP and URL.

Web Site – a collection of Web pages linked to a home page which is usually registered in a search engine so it can be found on the Web. From the home page, users can find other pages within the site.

Bibliography

If you're interested in learning more about the Internet and the Web, here are a few books (and one video) to get you started.

Weaving the Web: The Original Design and Ultimate Destiny of the World Wide Web by its Inventor
by Tim Berners-Lee (September 1999) Harper San Francisco; ISBN: 0062515861
Tim Berners-Lee invented the World Wide Web, and this is his story. There's no better place to start to get an idea of how the Web began and where its inventor would like it to go. A very interesting read.

Nerds 2.0.1: A Brief History of the Internet
by Bob Cringley, et al. (1999) ASIN: 6305128235
This three-tape video of the history of the Internet tells the story not just of the Web but of the Internet itself. It is quite entertaining, especially tapes one and three, and includes interviews with just about everyone who is anyone on the Web.

Architects of the Web: 1,000 Days That Built the Future of Business
by Robert H. Reid (February 1997) John Wiley & Sons; ISBN: 0471171875
By focusing on the characters whose creations shaped the Web, this book gives a behind-the-scenes look at the origins of the Web as well as such Web fixtures as Netscape, Yahoo, Hot Wired, Real Networks, and the Java programming language.

Internet Dreams: Archetypes, Myths, and Metaphors
by Mark J. Stefik, Vinton G. Cerf (September 1997) MIT Press; ISBN: 0262692023
A collection of thought-provoking essays that explore the idea that the way we think about the Internet will shape what it becomes.

And here are a few technical books for those who want to get into the details of HTML and graphics.

Building a School Web Site: A Hands-on Project for Teachers and Kids
by our very own Wanda Wigglebits (February 2001) Duomo Press; ISBN: 0967945631
Whether you're building a school, business, or personal Web site, this is a great, basic, easy and fun way to learn how to create Web sites. If you can follow a recipe, you can build a Web Site! Once you get the basics, you can move on to the books that follow.

Creating Web Pages With Html Simplified
by Ruth Maran (September 1999) IDG Books Worldwide; ISBN: 0764560670

Sams Teach Yourself Web Publishing with HTML 4 in 21 Days
by Laura Lemay, Denise Tyler (February 2000) Sams; ISBN: 0672318385

Designing Web Graphics.3
by Lynda Weinman (April 1999) New Riders Publishing; ISBN: 1562059491

Index

Access changing structure 145
ADSL 102, 103, 104
ADSL, definition 161
Affinity ISP 114
Andreessen, Marc 47, 48, 62, 73
Apollo 8 astronauts 13
Arbitrariness, inhibiting 152
Architects of the Web (Reid)
    123, 134
Art on the Web 50
ASCII 22, 23, 74
Asymmetric 104
Asymmetric Digital Subscriber Line
    102, 103
Asymmetric Digital Subscriber Line,
    definition 161
Atlas of Cyberspaces 96
Audio client 53, 54, 67
Audio file 53
Audio on demand 57
Audio player 53
Audio server 54
Awareness, increasing 156, 157

B2B 65
Backbone 95, 99, 106
Backbone, definition 161
Bandwidth
    60, 97, 98, 102, 104, 105
Bandwidth and capacity 97
Bandwidth and the world wide wait
    91
Bandwidth, definition 161
Bandwidth, importance 108, 109

Beckett, Sr. Wendy 50
Bell System 95, 107
Berners-Lee, Tim
    47, 73, 78, 86, 90, 101
Bit, definition 161
Bit maps 46
Bits 22, 24, 45, 67
Bits per second 98
Book, logic of 40
Book, manufactured object 40
Bottleneck 94, 102
Bps 98
Bps (bits per second), definition 162
Broadband
    101, 102, 103, 110, 111, 114, 118
Broadband, cost structures
    107, 108
Broadband, definition 162
Broadband, solutions 103
Broadcast, power of 110
Broadcasting Internet radio 58
Browser 26, 28, 29, 30, 33, 34
Browser, definition 162
Bundling 111, 114, 116, 118
Bundling, access and ISPs 113
Bundling, broadband 112
Bundling, content and connection
    113
Bundling, pricing issue 117
Bureaucracy, computers 152
Business-to-business 65

Cable ISP 105
Cable modem 105

169

Cable TV Internet access
  102, 103, 105, 108, 118
Cable TV Internet Access, definition
  162
Catalogs 83
CD ripper software 56, 77
Cell phone, broadband 107
Central office
  91, 92, 93, 102, 104
CGI 62
Chardin, Tielhard de 151
Client
  27, 28, 29, 30, 31, 34, 44, 54,
  67, 72, 92, 95
Client/Server, definition 162
Clients, smart 66, 125
Commentary, medieval manuscripts
  40
Commentary, Web 41
Common Gateway Interface 62, 63
Communication and exchange
  119, 121, 122, 124, 125, 127,
  142, 143
Communities of common interest
  134
Community, enhancing local
  136, 142
Community, formation of
  132, 133, 142
Community, Internet creation 138
Complex repositories of thought
  14, 42, 43, 68
Complexity 24, 41, 151
Complexity and transparency 140
Compression 47, 59
Compression, definition 163
Computers 22, 69, 71
  Bureaucracy 152
  Complexity 24, 122, 125
  Computation 26
  File 25
  Formalizing 152
  Illuminating 152
  Inhibiting arbitrariness 152
  Storage capacity 24, 122, 125
Content, shaping of 129, 134, 142
Context, awareness 156, 158
Context, epiphanies 155
Context, framework of meaning
  156
Convergence 108
Convergence, content and connection 115
Conversations, change 143
Conversations, enriched
  16, 25, 122, 123, 131, 134,
  142, 152, 159
Cooperation, power of 78
Copyleft 139
Copyright law 140, 146
Correspondence 133, 135
Culture of gifts 138
Cyberspace, Earth 141

Dancing hamsters 50
Dial-up 92, 93, 96, 103
Dial-up, definition 163
Digital 24, 29, 31, 44, 127
Digital Subscriber Line 112
Digitize 22, 108, 125
Digitize, definition 163
Digitized images 45, 46
Digitized sound 52
Digitized video 59
Digitized words 22, 23
Domain name 33, 81
Domain name, definition 163
Download 28, 66, 67, 94
Download, definition 163
Download time
  93, 96, 97, 104, 105
DSL 104, 112, 118
Dublin Core 88, 89

E-commerce 65
Embellishment, medieval manu-

INDEX

scripts 39
Embellishment, Web 41
Envisioning Information (Tufte) 49, 50
Epiphanies 155
Everyone's an operator 147
Exchange. *See* Communication and exchange

Fiber optics 106
File 25, 28, 29, 30, 31, 32, 33, 34, 44, 54, 67, 72, 95, 124, 125, 126
File, definition 163
File types 72
Files of logic 61
Files of pictures 45
Files of sound and motion 52
Files of words 35
Financial Accounting Standards Board 154, 155
Formalization 152, 155
Free software movement 139
Free speech vs. free beer 139
Freeware 55
Frequency range, copper wire 103, 104
Frequency range, human voice 103
Frequency range, telephone network 103
Friedman, Thomas 109, 155

G.lite 104
GIF 75
Giga 99
Gist 18
Giving back to the Web 138, 140
Global conversation 14, 43, 148, 150, 155
Global market 14
GNU General Public License 139
GNU software 139
Graphics Interchange Format 75

High-speed Internet access 93, 94, 96, 116
Hine, Lewis 49
Hosting 81
HTML 47, 73, 74, 75, 125
HTML, definition 163
HTTP 33, 47, 73, 74
HTTP, definition 163
Hyper Text Markup Language 73, 74
Hyper Text Markup Language, definition 163
Hyper Text Transfer Protocol 74
Hyper Text Transfer Protocol, definition 163
Hypertext 42, 43, 47, 131
Hypertext, definition 164

Illumination 152, 155
Image file guts 46
Individual, power of 14, 68
Infinite Diversity in Infinite Combinations 151
Information, formalization 152
Information, free flow 144
Information, illumination 152, 158
Integration of text and image, medieval manuscript 40
Integration of text and image, Web 41
Intellectual capital, amplifying 130, 142
Intellectual property 126
International Accounting Standards Committee 154
International Standards Organization 76, 153
Internet
  Awareness 157
  Changing concept of 31
  Definition 164
  Distributed processing 26
  Ethics 157

171

Flavor of text 41
Mass medium 36
Nature of 69
Network 91, 92, 95
Network of institutions 101
Power of 14, 43
Public network 115, 116
Radio 56, 125
Radio, broadcasting 58
Radio, control 58
Structure 95
Traffic
  25, 34, 94, 96, 100, 144
Visualizing 96
Internet Service Provider
  80, 91, 96, 111
Internet Service Provider, definition 164
Internet Society 72, 74, 95
Internet time 128
ISO 76
ISP 80, 81, 91, 95, 96, 101, 111, 112
ISP, affinity 114
ISP, choice 96, 105
ISP, content 113
ISP, definition 164
ISP, differentiation 114

Jobs, Steve 21
Joint Photographic Experts Group 75
JPEG 75
Judi 91, 108

Kilo 99

Link 33, 34, 42, 67
Link, definition 164
Link, web of connection 43
Linux operating system
  139, 140, 154, 155
LMDS 106

Local loop
  92, 93, 94, 102, 104, 106
Local loop, speeding up 100
Local Multipoint Distribution Services 106
Locke, Christopher 121, 149
Logic of the book 40
Logic, Web interface 63, 64
Lu, Cary 97

Marketplace, creation of 124, 148
Marketplace, market of one 149
Marketplace, price in 147
Martin, Henri-Jean
  35, 36, 39, 40, 44, 48, 130
Mega 99
Mesopotamia 37
Metadata 85, 86, 87, 88
Metadata Core Element Set 88
Metadata, definition 164
Metadata, real 88
Metadata, sort of 87
Middle C 103
MIME type 72
Modem
  91, 92, 93, 98, 100, 101, 102, 106
Modem, definition 164
Mosaic 48, 62
Mother of all paradigm shifts 150
Movable type 38, 109
MP3 54, 55, 76, 77, 125, 126, 146, 153
MP3 client 55
MP3 file 55, 56
MP3 player 55, 66
Multipurpose Internet Mail Extension 72

NAPs. See Network Access Points
National Service Providers
  95, 99, 100
Network Access Points 95, 99

172

INDEX

Network cashing 100
Network, definition 164
NGOs. *See* Non-governmental organizations
Niche audience 134
Non-governmental organizations 129, 146, 155
NSPs. *See* National Service Providers

On Photography (Sontag) 50
Open source 139, 140, 153
Open source movement 139, 155
Open standard, definition 164
Open standards 55, 59, 75, 153
Open standards, cooperation 78
Open standards, growth 77
Optical carrier 99
Optical carrier, definition 164
Oral tradition 39

Packet 32, 91, 95
Packet, definition 165
Paper 38, 109, 126
Papyrus 38
Parchment 38
PDF 125
Pera 99
Perabyte 97
Photographs 49
Pictures, coolness 47
Pinker, Steven 48
Pixel 46
Pixel, definition 165
Plug-in 29
Plug-in, definition 165
PNG 75
Pointcasting 57
POP3 75
Portable Network Graphic 75
Portals 83, 84
Post Office Protocol 3 75
Proprietary standard, definition 165

Proprietary standards 75
Public network 115
Public network, content neutral 115
Public network, ISP 115
Publishers Marketing Association 141, 144
Publishing, power of 123
Pull 81, 82, 90
Pull, definition 165
Push 82
Push, definition 165

QuickTime 55, 60, 97

RDF 88
RealAudio 76, 153
RealAudio file 54
RealPlayer 53, 54, 55, 60
Receiver 27, 28, 35, 56, 72
Reid, Robert 123, 134
Renaissance 38, 158
Renaissance yuppies 39
Request For Comments documents 74, 138
Resource Description Framework 88, 89
RFC 74, 138
Rheingold, Howard 133
Rippers. *See* CD ripper software
Roddenberry, Gene 151, 152
Rubrics, medieval manuscripts 40
Rubrics, Web 41

Sanity 158
Sanity, outbreak of 151
Satellite systems 106
Scribes 39
Scroll 38
Search Engines 83
Search for Extraterrestrial Intelligence 26
Semantic web 90
Sender 27, 28, 35, 56, 72

173

Server
   27, 28, 29, 30, 31, 33, 34, 44, 54, 67, 72, 92, 95
Server, definition 165
Servers, smart 62, 65, 125
SETI 26, 67
Shareware 55
Shovelware 58
Signal 27, 28, 32, 35, 56, 72
Simple Mail Transfer Protocol 75
Smart clients 66, 125
Smart servers 62, 65, 125
SMTP 75
Socratic dialog 129, 130
Software development business 67
Software, product vs. service 140
Solitary reader 39
Sontag, Susan 50
Sound file 52
Spider 84
Stallman, Richard 139
Standards, communication 71, 72
Standards, context and meaning 23, 72, 75, 156
Standards, file 73
Standards, open. *See* Open standards
Standards, open vs. proprietary 76
Standards organizations 74
Standards, proprietary. *See* Proprietary standards
Storage capacity 24, 41
Streaming 53, 59
Streaming audio 53, 54, 76
Streaming, definition 165
Streaming video 60, 125, 131

T1 98, 99
T1, definition 165
T3 99
T3, definition 165
TCP/IP 74
TCP/IP, definition 166

Telecommunications infrastructure 95, 118
Telephone company for computers 17, 19, 21, 30, 67, 93, 122, 159
Telephone network 27, 69, 71, 91, 93, 95, 104, 117, 122
Telephone network characteristics 93
Telephone wire 91, 92
Tera 99
The Cluetrain Manifesto (Locke) 121, 149
The History and Power of Writing (Martin) 35, 36, 44, 48, 130
The Language Instinct (Pinker) 48
The Lexus and the Olive Tree (Friedman) 109, 155
The Phenomenon of Man (Chardin) 151
The Race for Bandwidth (Lu) 97
The Visual Display of Quantitative Information (Tufte) 49
Transmission Control Protocol / Internet Protocol 74
Transmission Control Protocol / Internet Protocol, definition 166
Transparency 140, 153, 154, 155, 158
Transparency and complexity 140
Tufte, Edward 49, 50
Twisted pair 94

Uniform Resource Locator 33, 74
Uniform Resource Locator, definition 166
University of Illinois NSCA 48, 62
URL 33, 47, 53, 54, 57, 73, 74
URL, definition 166

Vectors 46
Video client 67
Video on the Web 59

INDEX

Virtual community 133, 135, 140
Virtual corporation 137
Visual Explanations (Tufte) 49
Visual knowledge 48
Visual knowledge, photographs
  49, 50
Visualizing discourse
  36, 41, 44, 127
Vulcan philosophy 151
Vulcans 151, 152

WAP 23
Weaving the Web (Berners-Lee)
  73, 78
Web, giving back to 138, 140

Web, human-machine 90
Web, power of 14, 68, 123
Web site, definition 166
Web, structure 95
Webcast 57, 131
What Is site 96
Wireless Access Protocol 23
Wireless options, broadband 106
World Wide Web, birth 73
World Wide Web Consortium
  73, 74, 75, 89, 96
World Wide Web, creation 47
World Wide Web, definition 166
Written word, common impulses 40

Additional copies of this book can be ordered via the Duomo Press Web site, http://www.duomopress.com

feedback: publisher@duomopress.com

Stafford Library
Columbia College
1001 Rogers Street
Columbia, Missouri 65216